**Capital Flows
in Minority
Areas**

Capital Flows in Minority Areas

John R. Dominguez
University of California,
Los Angeles

Lexington Books
D.C. Heath and Company
Lexington, Massachusetts
Toronto   London

CHICANO STUDIES LIBRARY
UNIVERSITY OF CALIFORNIA
BERKELEY, CALIFORNIA 94720

Library of Congress Cataloging in Publication Data

Dominguez, John R   1937–
    Capital flows in minority areas.

    Bibliography: p.
    Includes index.
    1. Minority business enterprises–United States
–Finance. 2. Capital–United States. 3. Finance–
United States. I. Title.
HD2346.U5D65   332'.041'0973   73–11669
ISBN 0–669–86926–0

Published simultaneously in Canada

Printed in the United States of America

International Standard Book Number: 0–669–86926–0

Library of Congress Catalog Card Number: 73–11669

To Tamara Martine, Our First Lady

Contents

List of Figures

List of Tables

Foreword

The literary and scholarly examinations of the treatment of minority and disadvantaged groups in American society have a crucial role in creating an awareness of the enormous inequities which have prevailed. These works are also forming the basis for the formulation of policies which, hopefully, will assist in the removal of these inequities. Professor John R. Dominquez of the University of California at Los Angeles has contributed to this important enterprise in this book by examining the functioning of financial institutions in relation to the economic life of American minorities. Turning over some of these pillared stone monuments of the United States economy, Dominquez finds an underground of business practices which, for American minorities, make this much less than the best of all possible worlds promised by the financial establishment.

The process of assessing the treatment of its minorities by American society, somewhat unexpectedly but now undoubtedly, is also helping to generate a better perception of its functioning with respect to the members of its white majority. Characteristically, for example, exposure of the inadequacies in the education of minority children and demands for reform have been followed by analogous demands for removal of the inequities in educational financing which are borne by white city residents.

This study by Dominguez documents the restrictive and discriminatory practices of financial institutions toward minority groups. But it takes little imagination to perceive that what is done on a broad scale to minorities must be similarly perpetrated on the white majority whenever possible. So the Dominguez study will help draw attention to all the urgent but relatively neglected problems of regulation of the competitive practices of financial institutions. Though the application to nonfinancial firms of the laws regulating monopoly and unfair competitive methods has been weak and inconsistent, such regulation has been virtually absent from the financial field with only few exceptions. Indeed it can be argued that state and federal policy regulatory policies for the financial sector have not only contributed substantially to the restraint of the interfirm competition which should protect the financial customer, but have not provided any other protection.

The Dominguez study also examines carefully the various federal programs which have attempted to supplement the financial flows from private institutions to minority communities. Though well intentioned, they too have had checkered careers. As Dominguez emphasizes, the heavy hand of the past continues to affect the ownership of wealth by minority groups. This, in turn, affects their ability to gain access to positions of ownership of enterprises. So programs intended to assist minorities in achieving these positions must be designed and evaluated differently than analogous programs for small business in general.

Economists, as yet, know relatively little about the implications of the operation of markets for the personal distribution of income. In some quite special conditions, which include perfect competition, there may be long run equalizing tendencies. But, as Dominguez shows, financial markets are not generally competitive and they do not operate to reduce income inequality. Moreover, the government programs designed to compensate for the deficiencies of private finance have, at best, been only moderately effective. Thus, American society continues to be faced with the question as to what financial institutions and procedures it will create to help its minorities achieve the citizenship parity which is Dominguez's criterion.

Richard S. Eckaus
September 1975

Preface

Throughout the history of Western civilization scholars have tried to express the activities of economic life and its institutions in terms of conventional propositions, traditional beliefs, and sacrosanct principles of the past. This has come to be known as economic thought. The stage of the arts, and the theories of optimization whether focusing on utility, efficiency, or equity, are all influenced by the social mores and the ideological preference of the established order. Because of the spatial-temporal nature of economic thought, its epistemological value may sometimes suffer from relative obsolescences. As Keynes succinctly stated in his celebrated work on the *General Theory of Employment Interest and Money:*

> The ideas of economist and political philosophers, both when they are right and they are wrong, are more powerful than is commonly understood. Indeed, the world is ruled by little else. Practical men, who believe themselves to be quite exempt from any intellectual influences are usually the slaves of some defunct economist. Madmen in authority who hear voices in the air are distilling their frenzy from some academic scribbler of a few years back.

Although Keynesian propositions are currently at a discount among members of the profession, it is evident his observation still has relevance. Recently, Sherman J. Maisel, giving his presidential address to the American Finance Association in 1973, noted that:

> Even though, in our theorems, we are normally cautious and point out potential costs when income distributions are changed in efforts to achieve possible improvements in efficiency, such strictures about the value judgments involved do not appear to have received much weight when these recommendations were made. But on the basis of considerable thought and analysis, I, at least believe it is highly probable that if the changes proposed in the financial structure are adopted in approximately their present form, they will be harmful. They will aggravate the instability of our economy; they will increase the inequality of income distribution and of sacrifice, and they will lead to a less efficient allocation of financial resources.

It is almost a prophetic outcome to find that in 1975 the average American family cannot obtain housing because of unavailable financial resources. New York City, which plays host to the largest financial center of the world, ironically finds itself facing imminent financial collapse and having to resort to demeaning hat-in-hand borrowing. What the rest of the nation is viewing is a situation which has historically prevailed in minority communities—this problem of having to cope with an existing financial system that systematically deprives segments of the population of necessary capital resources because of imperfections in the allocative market mechanism.

The purpose of this study has been to analyze the performance of financial markets and capital flows within the inner cities and the behavior of the institutions which are intended to facilitate intermediation. A corollary aim was to offer a basis for understanding the influence that the flow of funds has on the economic development of a minority area. This study is an outgrowth of the three year Ford Foundation project: Banking Activity and Capital Flows in Minority Areas: An Analysis of Mexican/American Ghetto Areas which extended from 1972–1975. The project was a two-sided effort aimed at ethnic community assistance and minority research. The first involved providing technical assistance and consultation to the minority business community, and the other was a series of empirical investigations aimed at determining how well or how poorly financial markets function in the *barrios* or ghettos of the economic disenfranchised. The project involved extensive amounts of field work and simulation studies and its sample sites were the states of California, Colorado, and Texas. During the tenure of the project, the author benefited from the comments and suggestions of the fifteen member project Advisory Board. Special thanks are gratefully extended to Professors Richard Eckaus, J. Fred Weston, Jacob Marschak, Fred E. Case, and to Dr. Henry Ramirez, previous Chairman, Cabinet Committee on Opportunities for the Spanish-Speaking, Dr. Marshall Robinson and Dr. Peter E. deJanosi of the Division of Higher Education and Research of the Ford Foundation for their sincere interest and the time they expended on behalf of the project. Another person who needs to be singled out for his unending commitment to the study from its inception to its culmination is Vice Chancellor Charles Z. Wilson. Without his support it is doubtful if the study would have advanced beyond the unanimated stage of the proposal. Financial support was also provided by the Ethnic and Urban Curriculum Grant which also made the publication of the study's findings possible. Several people spent arduous hours in field surveys, computer programming, research, editing and all those other countless tasks which unexpectedly arise and in some sense seem to confirm the pseudo-theory of spontaneous generation. Among this group, I wish to acknowledge debt to Divakar Kamath, Patricia Anderson, Kay Fujimoto, Janice Barnard, and Camilo Garcia. Thanks are also in order, as is

true with most authors, to my editor-in-residence, my wife, Karen Jeanne
Darcy Dominguez, whose professional efforts once again got me past this
last hurdle.

1 The Function of Financial Markets

Everyone individual is continually exerting himself to find out the most advantageous employment for whatever capital he can command. It is his own advantage, indeed, and not that of the society, which he has in view. But the study of his own advantage naturally, or rather necessarily, leads him to prefer that employment which is most advantageous to the society.

Adam Smith, 1802[1]

Introduction

A modern, industrially oriented economy requires a financial market system that is responsive to the varying needs of its households, firms, and governmental agencies. The function of a financial system is to link savings, particularly those derived from the growth of modern sectors of the economy, with the investment needs of business enterprises. A well-functioning capital market system is important to a growing community because the positive growth of a population and its personal income requires continuous support from efficient financial intermediaries.

As a community's standard of living rises and the capacity to save increases, the need for financial intermediation between savers and investors increases. The capacity of a community to invest, and hence to expand its economic activity in the long run, depends on the existence of efficiently functioning financial flows. Thus, a primary characteristic of an efficient financial system is its ability to supply financial resources that are sufficient to support increased economic growth in a growing community.

A second related characteristic of a well-functioning capital market is that it insures optimum allocation of available resources among all the sectors that require financing: business enterprises, housing facilities, public goods, and the various community needs within these sectors.

Capital and Its Definitions

Capital is a word that has various interpretations. Most of its meanings usually imply that capital is a stock, in contrast to income, which is a flow.

1

Capital may be broadly defined as the set of economically significant elements in existence at a moment in time. The various concepts and definitions of capital therefore revolve around the question of defining what is semantically appropriate. In its broadest sense, capital includes nonmaterial elements such as skills, abilities, education, health of the population, as well as land, buildings, machines, equipment of all types and vintages, and all finished or unfinished goods in the hands of both the private and public sectors.

Within the discipline of economics, the term capital is traditionally restricted to real physical, as opposed to merely financial, assets. In the field of finance, the term usually refers to an item in the balance sheet which represents that part of the net worth of an enterprise that is not accrued through the operations of the enterprise. As different as the two concepts may seem, they are interrelated. If all balance sheets were consolidated in a closed economic system, all debts would be cancelled out because every debt is an asset in one balance sheet and a liability in another. The consolidated balance sheet would contain the value of all the real assets of a society on one side, and total net worth on the other. This is the economist's concept of capital.

In the field of finance, the term may denote various accounting entries that may or may not relate to man-made goods destined for further use in production. In its most basic use, the term capital is associated with capital structure. This is the permanent long-term financing of a firm, which corresponds to long-term debt, preferred stock, and net worth. Capital structure is distinguished from "financial structure" in that the latter includes short-term debt plus all reserve accounts.

The meanings of other terms involving capital also differ according to the discipline using them. In fiscal policy, capital budgeting means separating government expenditures into current expenditures, financed by taxation over a long term, and developmental expenditures, financed through long-term borrowing. However, in finance this means the process of planning expenditures on assets whose returns are expected to extend over a year. Capital stock also has more than one meaning. In finance, it means net worth and the total shares of a corporation, while in economics, it means the total amount of all produced goods in existence.[a]

---

[a]Other common uses of the concept of capital are: *capital asset:* an asset with a life of more than one year that is not bought and sold in the ordinary course of operation; *capital goods:* man-made goods destined for use in further production, i.e., machines and raw materials; *capital market:* financial market for long-term funds; *capital rationing:* a situation in which a constraint is placed on the total size of the capital investment during a given period; *capital consumption:* the depreciation of a firm's capital assets during a period. As is apparent from the semantic latitude of the word "capital" and its variety of applications, it is probably necessary to state that "capital flows" in the context of this study will mean short-, intermediate-, and long-term purchasing power claims; the term will only on occasion be restricted to the traditional economic sense of the stock of capital goods, such as plant, equipment, and inventories; when used in this manner, a clear indication will be given.

Capital Flows and Financial Markets

Within a closed system capital flows may be viewed as a transfer of funds from one community to another. This command over purchasing power may be exchanged between individuals, firms, financial institutions, governments, or nonprofit organizations. The motives behind capital transfers include: credit provisions for financing trade transactions, speculative purchase or sale of real estate property in anticipation of an increase or decrease in its market value, the earning of interest or dividends generated outside of the community, and governmental subsidy supports. The primary motive for transferring capital is to change command over goods and services or assets.

There are various categories used for describing capital movements. Some of the categories are: stabilizing and destabilizing movements, depending upon whether they tend to restore or move away from their equilibrium values; autonomous and induced movements, depending upon whether they initiate or respond to exogenous or endogenous disturbances; and normal and abnormal movements, depending upon whether or not they move from a capital-poor to a capital-rich community. The most typical division, however, is between short- and long-term movements. Short-term movements are embodied in credit instruments maturing in less than one year. Long-term capital movements are longer than one year. They usually include mortgage, debenture and convertible debt, preferred stock, government loans and direct subsidies, or hybrid instruments, such as warrants or letter stock.

At this point, it may be helpful to review the differences between finance and product markets. First, a distinction is usually made between financial markets and markets for real goods and services, since in the former, transactions involve only claims on money, goods, and services. However, the distinction between the two markets is not always clear. For example, in standardized commodity markets, contracts for future delivery of goods are often sold without buyer or seller having any intention of taking or making delivery.

Secondly, financial institutions issue indirect securities that are traded on financial markets. Simultaneously, firms and households, which produce and purchase goods and services, issue primary securities for the same markets. Some financial markets, like the stock exchanges, specialize almost entirely in primary securities, while the "money market" specializes in an exchange of financial claims for claims.

In most cases, the money market is seen as corresponding to the market for short-term debt instruments with a maturity or a year or less. The capital market, on the other hand, is viewed as involving long-term debt or equity commitments. There is also another category, which is intermediate-term funding. This corresponds to 1-to-5, or 1-to-10-year maturities. Throughout the discussion which follows, transactions involving intermediate-term instruments will be included in our concept of capital flows.

**The Evolution and Performance
of Financial Centers**

The schools of urban and regional economics examine the location of commerce, industry, and housing, but seldom do they discuss banking and the formation of financial centers and their role in economic development. Also, what literature there is on the subject makes little mention of geographical location or the relationships between financial centers. Much of this literature would lead the reader to think that money and capital were distributed evenly throughout the country, rather than pooled in a few financial centers. In spite of its neglect in the literature, the geography of finance is relevant to contemporary issues and of considerable historical interest. Its contemporary relevance is evident in the similar financial needs of developing countries and minority communities.

Financial centers are needed to balance through time the savings of households and investments of firms, to affect payments, and to transfer savings between points in space. Financial centers perform a medium-of-exchange and store-of-value function. Under normal conditions, payment flows between different communities are facilitated by financial centers. Seasonal and resource surpluses and deficits of savings are coordinated and allocated by centers.

As an efficient system of payments develops utilizing the exchange function of banking, firms are able to economize on working balances by centralizing in a metropolitan city. Large companies, upon reaching a certain size, tend to establish financial offices in metropolitan centers in order to operate in geographically separated financial markets as well as to finance a larger flow of funds with smaller working balances. This is followed by the development of competitive security markets which provide larger and cheaper security issues for firms that need long-term financing as well as a more liquid investment instrument for lenders. Also, as financial markets develop, they begin to experience economies of scale in the store-of-value and medium-of-exchange functions.

The function of the financial markets has evolved from its institutional setting for linking resource exchange between demand and supply forces. The fundamental performance characteristic of financial markets is the transfer of purchasing power from one entity to another. It is not necessary that it involve a physical transfer of currency or of financial assets, and it may register itself simply as a double-entry accounting notation on a set of credit-debit ledgers. The flow of funds within this context is an exchange of financial claims between one economic unit and another.

These claims can be classified in accordance to the type of associated ownership, such as assets, liabilities, or equity. When financial markets are working properly, they directly facilitate exchange of asset, debt, and equity instruments, and indirectly enhance the exchange of goods and services, which can include factor inputs and intermediate and final products. This trichotomous array of claims may serve as a store of value and as a medium of exchange.

The organizational structure of financial markets may vary from monopolistic forms, such as central banking systems, to monopolistic competitors, such as Minority Enterprise Small Business Investment Companies (MESBICs), to differentiated oligopolists, as in the case of commercial banks and savings and loan associations. The type of organization and market structures will determine how efficiently a financial market clears its surpluses and deficits, as well as the flexibility and stability of its price adjustments. Under ideal competitive conditions, if there are demand-supply inequalities, financial markets will at any given point in time or space create a set of interacting forces for bringing into balance the exchange equation. Ideal performance occurs when a market adjusts smoothly and quickly, and it entails the least economic cost to the host community. Financial resource exchange may involve a single transaction between an individual unit of demand and a single unit of supply, or a combination of single-multiple or multiple-multiple exchange mappings. In a one-on-one mapping, a demand entity is interacting with the single supply entity, and either may represent units of the public or private sector. In the multiple exchange mapping, a consortium of borrowers or lenders is interacting in the market place. The degree to which supply-demand units can combine with one another will often determine the relative size of financial transactions and affect the level of competition. For example, in commercial banking, the size of the bank is an important determinant of its lending capacity, since the maximum amount that an individual bank may lend to any single borrower is limited to 10 percent of the bank's capital account (which is its capital stock plus its surplus accounts). Given this regulatory constraint, a consortium of lenders or borrowers permits by-passing of this regulation.

In 1971, nine minority banks formed a consortium in order to extend legally a one million dollar line of credit to Levi Strauss and Company, based in San Francisco, and one of the largest apparel manufacturers. The group included Seaway National Bank, Chicago; Industrial Bank of Washington, D.C.; Liberty Bank of Seattle; Freedom National Bank of New York City; Tri State Bank of Memphis; First Independence National Bank, Detroit; North Milwaukee State Bank; Bank of Finance, Los Angeles; and First Plymouth National Bank, Minneapolis.

In general, consortia may be established in order to permit financial institutions to enjoy a greater volume of a particular activity, or to avoid regulation. The Interbank system, which eventually assumed the operations of California's Mastercharge, was made up of a consortium of banks which included Citizens and Southern in Atlanta, Bank of Virginia in Richmond, First Wisconsin in Milwaukee, Valley National in Phoenix, Seattle First, and First Louisville Bank. Similarly, multinational banks have established consortia in order to expand their intermediate-term lending activities. Additionally, by organizing as a consortium, financial institutions can side-step the controls of central banks of the parent holding companies, which normally could be exercised over a wholly-owned foreign subsidiary or branch. A case in point is the current situation in which the Federal Reserve has no regulatory power over a consortium. A U.S. bank may participate in conjunction with lending institutions from other countries. For example, the Société Financière Européene (SFE), organized in Paris and Luxembourg in 1967, includes Barclays Bank, Ltd. (Britain), Banca Nazionale del Lavoro (Italy), Bank of America, N.T. & S.A. (United States), and Banque Nationale de Paris (France).

Similar circumstances may also be found in the field of investment banking, in which multiple participation by equity underwriters is necessary in order to offer publicly a new security issue.

The establishment of prices in the financial markets creates a series of intertemporal and interspatial values that provides borrowers and lenders a basis for discerning relative benefits and costs for making rational economic decisions. Each market participant is confronted with a set of alternative sources and uses, corresponding to a vector of prices. Equilibrium is achieved when each individual cannot improve his gains or reduce his losses by any other combination of alternatives than his exercised choice. It is within this trade-off that decisions are made which determine the optimal allocation of financial resources. It is this underlining structure of a financial market and its allocation mechanism which ensures a balance between the vectors of supply and demand, and subsequently determines the Samuelsonian trilogy of what is produced, how it is produced, and for whom.

Relation between Finance and Development

For some time there has been an expressed interest in the relationship between finance and development. This has evolved from the belief that there is a positive relationship between financial structure and economic development. Baumol singles out the importance of capital resources to economic well-being. According to Baumol:

> The allocation of its capital resources is among the most important decisions which must be made by any economy. In the long run an appropriate allocation of real capital is absolutely indispensable to the implementation of consumer sovereignty (or of the more appropriate concept—public sovereignty—which takes into account *all* of the relevant desires of the individuals who constitute the economy). For unless the flow of capital goods is responsive to the goals of the members of the public, the community will only be able to exercise a very short-run and temporary control over the composition of output and of its activities. After all, capital is the economy's link with the future and unless our desires can influence the apportionment of capital inputs, our wishes can at most effectively control only today's events.[2]

Also, capital resources allocation is crucial to determining the rate at which national output increases. The economy's growth will definitely be impeded if capital is not made available for research and development, to those sectors capable of increasing productivity, and to those industries whose products are in increasing demand. Economic growth will also be adversely affected if the capital allocation mechanism is not flexible and quickly responsive to public wishes; this mechanism has a direct effect upon the adaptability of the production mechanism and thus upon the entire economy.

The allocation of real capital among individual firms and industries, and the form of this capital, is controlled essentially by the funds market. Therefore, decisions of the nation's financial institutions strongly influence the allocation mechanism. Similarly, securities markets, particularly stocks and bonds markets, and governmental monetary policies help determine the apportionment of real capital.

Baumol sees a crucial relationship existing between financial markets and real capital formation. He states that:

> ... the selection of the physical forms which constitute the embodiment of our capital resources is largely controlled through the funds market— the market on which *money* capital is provided. Thus the allocation process is heavily influenced by the decisions of the nation's financial institutions, its banks, its insurance companies, and a variety of other bodies many of which will come to mind immediately. In addition the government's monetary and fiscal policies obviously play a highly important role in a variety of ways which need not be gone into here.[3]

On the other hand, Eckaus has noted:

> That belief, however, is not grounded firmly either on factual observation or *a priori* argument. It is true that there appears to be empirical associations between financial development and economic growth.[4]

In a historical investigation of the development of financial centers, Kindleberger found that earlier studies by Hoselitz, Gerschenkron, and more recently, Cameron, had attempted to answer the question by specifically examining the role of banking in economic development.[5] Cameron's work involved the analysis of certain European countries' banking institutions through a series of case studies.

Cameron's conclusions were that the influence of banking on economic development depends mostly on the structural characteristics, governing laws and regulations, and customs of the system, rather than on the merits of the individual bank or its policies. The studies of Cameron and the other men have a parallel approach in that they attempt to answer the question of causality by examining the effects of banking on economic growth, via the stimulation of demand.

Other works by Van Horne, Shaw, and Goldsmith have focused their attention on the economic benefits of financial intermediation through the mobilization and allocation of funds. Van Horne succinctly states,

> The purpose of financial markets is to allocate savings efficiently in an economy to ultimate users, either for investment and real assets or for consumption.[6]

Viewed in this way, a financial matrix is an all-inclusive universe. Borrowing and lending institutions, which act to bring together borrowers and lenders of all types, are exhaustive subsets of the universe. Van Horne goes on to say,

> Efficient financial markets are absolutely essential to assure adequate capital formation and economic growth in a modern economy.[7]

As viewed by Van Horne, finance plays a crucial role in determining national and local levels of economic development. Shaw begins his recent work on the same subject with the following argument.

> The financial sector of an economy does matter in economic development. It can assist in the break-away from plodding repetition of repressed economic performance to accelerated growth. If it is repressed and distorted, it can intercept and destroy impulses to development.[8]

The financial sector complements and positively stimulates the rate of economic growth as long as the ratio of financial assets and nonfinancial wealth to total output is not less than unity, or stated differently, as long as the development strategy is not directed toward *shallow finance*. Shaw's financial liberalization can lead towards financial deepening, can correct the movement of real interest rates by inducing the substitution of capital-intensive for labor-intensive methods of output, and by providing increments to savings. Further, if the elasticity of substitution between labor and capital is greater than unity, then increases in the cost of capital will lead to increases in the labor share of income.[9]

A well-behaved financial sector is the important lubricant for capital formation and sustained economic growth. The mobilizing of savings and the channeling of funds into capital markets is an important element in the development process. Shaw regards financial institutions and capital markets as more vital to economic development than export expansion or foreign aid.

Goldsmith follows suit by stating that:

> The financial superstructure in the form of both primary and secondary securities, accelerates economic growth and improves economic performance to the extent that it facilitates the migration of funds to the best users, i.e., to the place in the economic system where the funds will find the highest social return.[10]

Notwithstanding, Goldsmith does qualify his statement by stating:

> The result thus is the same whether we turn to economic theory or to economic history, possibly because there is after all some communication between the two fields. Both assure us that the existence and development of a superstructure of financial instruments and financial institutions is a necessary, though not a sufficient, condition of economic growth, and both point out that the relationships between financial development and economic growth are very complicated and not easily amenable to generalization. Both however fail to answer the question in which we are primarily interested: Does finance make a difference, i.e., are there historically observed or theoretically inferred differences in the speed and pattern of economic development that are the result primarily, even if not exclusively, of differences in financial structure and development?[11]

Shaw identifies development with liberalized finance. Financing production and trade *pari passu* to the prevailing return on real assets positively influences economic development. Integration and liberalization of capital markets eliminates local and sectoral monopoly and monopsony, which permits superior allocation of savings by diversifying and widening the financial markets in which investment opportunities compete for the flow of savings. He cites that the market for savings can be broadened and local capital markets can be integrated into a consolidated market in order to create new opportunities for pooling savings and to allow for investment specialization. McKinnon, in a study whose theme resembles Shaw's, stresses the importance of increasing the rate of interest on financial resources to equal the cost of real capital. This encourages entrepreneurs to save funds for future investments, and increases the availability of external financial capital, enabling entrepreneurs, who would otherwise be limited to their own saving capacity, to start ventures sooner and on a larger scale.[12]

Gunnar Myrdal, however, sees capital market consolidation and liberalization as having other consequences. In societies in which there are extreme regional differences in industrial activity, there will be a general tendency for capital to migrate to the richer areas, thus causing a "backwash effect" that would tend to lessen investment in poorer regions of the economy.

> It is easy to see how expansion in one locality has "backwash effects" in other localities. More specifically the movements of labour, capital, goods and services do not by themselves counteract the natural tendency to regional inequality. By themselves, migration, capital movements and trade are rather the media through which the cumulative process evolves—upwards in the lucky regions and downwards in the unlucky ones. In general, if they have positive results for the former, their effects on the latter are negative. . . . Capital movements tend to have a similar effect of increasing inequality. In the centres of expansion increased demand will spur investment, which in its turn will increase incomes and demand and

cause a second round of investment, and so on. Saving will increase as a result of higher incomes but will tend to lag behind investment in the sense that the supply of capital will steadily meet a brisk demand for it. In the other regions the lack of new expansionary momentum has the implication that the demand for capital for investment remains relatively weak, even compared to the supply of savings which will be low as incomes are low and tending to fall. Studies in many countries have shown how the banking system, if not regulated to act differently, tends to become an instrument for siphoning off the savings from the poorer regions to the richer and more progressive ones where returns on capital are high and secure.[13]

In addition to this "backwash effect" there are certain side effects from capital shortages. If a community continues to experience a capital bypass, the outcome will be a further decrease in the level of economic activity due to the limited potential for technological improvements as a result of lack of "capital widening" or "capital deepening."

Probing further into the issue, Eckaus points out that:

> There are two rationalizations which are customarily used to relate financial development and economic growth: (1) such development will improve the collection or mobilization of saving and (2) such development will improve the allocation of investment resources. Occasionally there is the suggestion there is empirical evidence supporting one or both of the arguments in any case. Each of these rationalizations is usually regarded as more or less self-evident. They are repeated at the outset of most discussions relating the evolution of capital markets and financial instruments to development. Yet after homage is paid to the ideas, they are seldom, if ever, discussed in depth though they are continually cited as the justification for innovations which would increase the sophistication of the financial markets.[14]

A testimonial from a representative of the finance industry serves to illustrate this point of view. Cleveland A. Christophe of the First National City Corporation asserted:

> The public benefit requires that the nation's financial services sytem be effective, efficient, flexible, and sound. To achieve the highest level of economic prosperity, sterile funds surpluses must be used to finance economic activity and to fund the formation of productive resources and other capital assets. Consumers, governments, and business concerns each depend upon the availability of such funds to sustain levels of economic activity beyond those supportable by their immediate internal funds-generating capabilities. An effective financial system adequately provides for fund flows from accumulators to worthy users. An efficient system operates at minimal internal cost, while optimizing the benefit-cost

ratio to system users. A flexible system is properly responsive to new and
increasing demands placed upon it by socioeconomic change. And a
sound system is comprised of well-managed, fiscally-healthy institutions
which through profitable operations serve the public's needs without
requiring public subsidization, either in the form of direct money subsidies or protective legislation and regulation.[15]

Within this practitioner's view, the function of financial markets is to provide the
public with the best service at the lowest cost that the market place can provide.
The system best able to provide this service at low cost is the free market system;
it is still the most effective economic system yet constructed for providing the
greatest number of consumers with the greatest good. Institutions operating within the free market system serve and affect many sectors: governments, competitors, stockholders, employees, and customers. Since the interests of these
sectors are not identical, it is necessary to identify the sector that will receive
prime consideration. Every individual and corporate citizen is ultimately a customer, so the customer sector is the largest and should receive favored status.
Indeed, the financial system exists to serve customers. Thus, the efficacy of a
financial system may perhaps be best evaluated in terms of how well it achieves
a state of customer sovereignty.

    At this point Christophe makes a distinction between the different types of
customers: borrowers, investors, savers, insurers, and other clients. Customers
may be further differentiated according to scale of service required, and to
nature—individual or corporate. Regardless of these considerations, each must
be served effectively and efficiently if the public interest is to be met. Both
consumer and corporate small borrower should be able to find competitive
lenders who offer funds at the best possible interest rates for small transactions.
Individual savers and large corporations alike should receive a market rate of
interest on their accumulated funds. And prospective home buyers should not
be prevented from borrowing because of the limitation of funds caused by over-
specialization and interest rate ceilings.

    Christophe continues his argument by stating that,

    The probability of attaining these standards, and hence a viable financial
    system, is greatest in a free-market, relatively unrestrained environment
    where the forces of fair competition arbitrate between a financial in-
    stitution's success or failure. Alternatively, when competition is not
    allowed to induce responsiveness or failure upon market entrants, the
    inevitable result is a decline in the system's effectiveness, efficiency,
    and flexibility.[16]

Presumably the present status quo is a close approximation of the type of
financial structure which is conducive to prosperity and growth. Judging from
Christophe's preference for a reinstatement of a laissez-faire system of finance,

financial markets would asymptotically approach perfection if regulation were reduced to a minimum. Though a comprehensive rationalization, this mercantilistic dictum does not lead to further insight into the causal relationship between finance and development. It seems that part of the problem is semantic, and the other part is attributable to reliance on qualitative inferences to determine effects of financial flows on economic development.

Eckaus focuses on this by asking the question:

> Well then, what is financial development? It is seldom if ever, well-defined. Goldsmith calls it simply, "change in financial structure." But then goes on to argue that there is a more or less common pattern to such change which is followed by countries in the course of their growth. With customary caution he abjures an opinion as to whether this pattern is a necessary one and itself contributes to economic development. Yet, while the descriptions of financial structures remain qualitative and their relations to economic development remain unspecified, it is impossible to assess the significance of the variability in financial patterns which do exist. The most pressing task, therefore, is to identify the various contributions which financial structure can make to economic development generally. The next step would be to try to develop quantitative measures or indicators of this contribution as the way to begin to formulate policy for financial change.[17]

This is a question of significance, but it is doubtful that an unequivocal answer to the question is within our limitations due to its absolutely dichotomous nature. Relationships, like individuals, will vary through time and space. The relation between financial structure and economic development may well be positive, negative, or zero, depending on the influences of other interacting variables, such as institutional and governmental barriers of socioeconomic discrimination, human and physical resource endowment, and market concentration. The relevant question then is: Under what conditions do we have a positive relationship between financial structure and growth, and how does this relationship weaken as we move through time and space? From this starting point we should be able to determine and measure the true population parameters in order to understand, control and predict the effects of this kinship.

Market Structure

The structure of financial markets may be defined in several different ways. A narrow definition of market structure may be based on a purely quantitative analysis which considers such factors as the number and size distribution of financial institutions within a specified market area. The boundaries of the market may be designated as local (cities, SMSAs, or counties), regional (partial,

single, or multi-state), and national (several, most or all states). A broader definition of structure would include other features such as the number and the size
distribution of borrowers and lenders and their respective influence on conditions. A comprehensive definition of structure, by its very nature, should include
all principal factors that influence market performance. If a financial instrument
is without a reasonable substitute and is traded between independent, well-
informed lenders and borrowers, then the two structural elements that will have
the most effect on the degree of market competition and the volume of transactions for any given firm are the number and the relative size of borrowers and
lenders, and the actual and potential freedom of entry of new competitors.
Other corollary conditions are the relative autonomy between markets and zero
differences in initial capital outlay for market entry. In the short run, *ceteris
paribus,* the number and size of the market participants are the key variables
that influence market structure, whereas in the long run, free entry and exit,
assuming the previous conditions cited, are the determining factors.

Historically, the finance, insurance, and real estate industries are the industries in which minority firms have their poorest representation.[b] The structure
of minority financial markets is a modest cluster of small interdependent firms.
These firms, by any conventional standard, have minimal economic visibility,
whether comparisons are made between their relative number *vis à vis* the industry, the relative size of their asset-financial structure and the volume of their
receipts, or their representative sample and the respective size of their population
constituency.

In some respects the commercial banking industry serves to illustrate many
of these disproportionalities. In 1972 there were 13,472 commercial banks.
These intermediaries serve as depositors and coordinators of this country's
demand deposit payment system and are the primary sources of short- and
intermediate-term financing. They also play a pivotal role in the development
and viability of other financial institutions.[c]

The structure of the banking industry with respect to asset size of individual
firms resembles the Rabelaisian extreme of Gargantua and Pantagruel. At the end
of 1974, the Bank of America recorded assets of $60.4 billion, as compared to
nearly a thousand banks which had less than one million in deposits each year.
We can only begin to appreciate this size disparity when we consider that even if
we took one portion of Bank of America asset structure, which would in effect
amount to 15 times the total asset value of all minority firms, we would still be
able to completely absorb the nominal value of the Gross National Product of
Mexico.

---

[b]Real estate industry participation will be discussed in chapter 5.
[c]Those institutions whose operational performance depends on the activities of the
banking industry are savings and loans, mutual savings, mortgage banking companies, insurance companies, real estate investment trusts, and consumer finance companies.

Among the ranks of the banking industry, 41 institutions could be identified as minority-owned.[d] In percentage terms, this constitutes only a fraction of a fraction of the number of banks within the industry—approximately 0.3 percent. Their relative shares of total assets and deposits are also marginal. Total assets and deposits for the commercial banking industry amounted to $746.1 and $621.5 billion, respectively. The per capita asset and deposit holdings for the average bank amounted to $53.5 and $44.6 million.

For minority banks, total assets and deposits came to $676.9 and $596.2 million. The asset and deposit holdings for the average bank amounted to $14.5 and $16.5 million per bank. The stock of assets and deposits held by minority-owned banks represents an even smaller fraction of total industry representation. Minority banks accounted for 0.096 percent and 0.091 percent of the 1972 industry asset-deposit totals. By the end of 1974, six more banks were added to the minority listing and the combined assets of this banking segment still accounted for less than one-tenth of 1 percent of the total assets of all commercial banks. The asset and deposit mean ratios show less disparate relationships. The average minority bank's asset structure is one-fourth the size of the average commercial bank, and its deposit structure approximately one-third.

Without getting into the bias shortcomings of per capita figures,[e] on face value this can be interpreted as implying that minority lending institutions have not been able to attract and mobilize an adequate volume of deposits, nor have they been able to provide the necessary resource level for channeling investment funds into minority communities. Much of this is due to the circumstances that

---

[d]The reader should be cautioned that there are different estimated figures for the number of minority commercial banks. For example, in John Boorman's study, *New Minority-Owned Commercial Banks: A Comparative Analysis* (Washington, D.C.: Federal Deposit Insurance Corporation, 1973), p. 47, there is a listing from the Federal Deposit Insurance Corporation which shows 41 minority banks in operation by the end of 1972. The U.S. Department of Commerce, Office of Minority Business Enterprise, released a different estimate which was compiled by an OMBE Local Business Development Organization, the Chicago Economic Development Corporation. It showed that the minority banks amounted to 65. See *Access,* published by the OMBE, U.S. Department of Commerce (July–August, 1973), p. 8. A similar difference for the year 1969 has been observed in comparing the minority bank figure compiled by Brimmer from data of the Controller of the Currency, the Federal Reserve Board, and the F.D.I.C. He estimates there were 22 minority banks in 1969. See Andrew Brimmer, "The Black Banks: An Assessment of Performance and Propsects," *Journal of Finance Papers and Proceedings,* Volume 26, No. 2 (May 1971), p. 380. However, the Bureau of the Census of the U.S. Department of Commerce estimates that for the same year there were 62 institutions which came under the category of "banking." Nineteen of these banks were listed as not having paid employees. This seems to be a sample classification error. Or there is a definitional difference between the commercial banking regulatory agencies and the U.S. Department of Commerce. The Bureau of the Census did not define "banking" in its publication. See *Minority-Owned Businesses: 1969* MB-1, Bureau of the Census, U.S. Department of Commerce (August 1971), p. 12.

[e]As stated, there are certain reservations one should exercise in the use and interpretation of per capita figures. For instance, a per capita value is in itself an average. It does not tell us how much above or below some lending institutions may be with respect to the mean. Similarly, it does not disclose how many banks are near the per capita figure.

minority banks are usually hosted in low income and wealth areas and that minority institutions are bypassed by the capital allocative mechanism, of the existing financial system.

The savings and loan industry is another industry that provides depository facilities and a flow of funds on a national basis. Up until recent times, savings and loans (S & Ls) were mostly located in the western part of the United States instead of displaying a uniform geographical dispersion. Savings and loans of a "stock" type were restricted to only twenty states. By the end of 1972, a state census showed S & Ls had offices in every state of the union, and in the District of Columbia, Puerto Rico, and Guam. Seven states—Pennsylvania (552), Illinois (527), Ohio (461), New Jersey (296), Texas (282), Maryland (229) and California (182)—accounted for almost half of the country's savings and loans.[18]

Savings and loan associations operating under federal charter numbered 2,044 and recorded a total asset structure of $135.9 billion, which constituted 55.8 percent of the total assets of the savings and loan industry. In the same year, 1972, state chartered mutuals made up 3,404 firms and had $107.7 billion in total assets, which represented 44.2 percent of the industry asset share, but accounted for 62.5 percent of the total number of S & Ls. The total industry numbered 5,448 firms with a total resource value of $243.6 billion.

In 1972 there were 60 chartered minority savings and loan associations with assets of approximately $500 million. By the end of 1974, this number had increased to 72. Minority savings and loans represented 1.1 percent of the S & L industry. Their respective total asset position approximated the equivalent value which was true for minority banks—one-tenth of 1 percent. However, the disproportion is greater since there is a larger number of minority S & Ls than minority commercial banks.

The asset structure of the average S & L amounted to $44.6 million. In contrast, the total assets of the average minority S & L was one-sixth the size of its industry counterpart, $6.7 million. Usually the savings deposit to asset ratio will vary between 80 and 85 percent. This can be interpreted as implying that the average minority S & L will attract annually between $5.4 and $5.7 million, whereas the range for the industry is between $35.6 and $37.9 million.

Twelve minority *de novo* S & Ls were expected by the end of 1974 and with this increase in the number of firms, it was projected that total assets for the group would climb to $420 million. If this 5 percent asset growth rate is indicative of the average firm, then we can expect that it will not be until after A.D. 2000 that the average minority S & L would achieve asset parity.[f] However, this is at best a wishful underestimate, since this assumes that the industry

---

[f]This exponential growth path assumes the proportionality factor between the number of firms and total assets remains constant. This may not be a safe assumption since in moving from 1973 to 1974 we observe a decrease in the per capita asset holding from $6.67 in 1973 to $5.83 million in 1974. If this type of asset dilution continued without counterbalancing asset scale economies, then we could rightfully expect that the above estimated time horizon is an understatement of when minorities would achieve industry parity.

per capita figure for 1972 remains constant throughout the period. In fact, the asset structure for the average firm over the previous eight years (1965-1973) had been steadily increasing at a rate of 12.27 percent per annum. We can conclude from this that the gap between average asset holdings of minority savings and loan associations will enlarge in decades to come, unless minority firms can more than double their per captia growth rate.

The Mortgage Bankers Association roster shows that the number of mortgage banking firms has been decreasing over the years since the 1950s. This is at least partially due to the general trend towards larger firms; there have been a significant number of horizontal mergers. According to some rough estimates, 62 of the firms were acquired by other mortgage companies in the 1963-1969 period, and most companies that resigned from membership in the Mortgage Bankers Association were small firms.[19]

Of the 742 mortgage banking companies in 1972, 33 were Black companies whose total portfolio servicing volume amounted to $90 million. Thus, minority enterprises account for 4 percent of the number of mortgage banking firms. Their portfolio servicing volume annually represents less than three-tenths of 1 percent of the volume generated by all mortgage banking companies.

According to figures released by the U.S. Department of Commerce Bureau of the Census, there were 178 insurance carriers in 1969, whose gross revenues amounted to $135.8 million.[g] Of this group, 61 percent did not have any paid employees, and the average gross receipts per firm amounted to $23,000 annually. These firms without employees, although accounting for a little less than two-thirds of the number of minority insurance carriers, shared less than 2 percent of the revenue.

There were 70 firms with paid employees. These companies had typically staff levels of 60 employees per firm. The yearly per capita receipt for this group was $1.1 million, and the average revenue product of its employees was $32,000 per year. Each employee was able to generate five time as much revenue as the single proprietor operated carriers. Thus, there is no question that there are definite economies of scale once you penetrate far enough beyond the poverty threshold, which is evident from the fact that companies with employees were able to generate 47 times as much revenue.

Minority insurance companies can be traced back to 1899, when North Carolina Mutual was established. Historically, they began by providing burial insurance, and as time progressed, they began offering ordinary life insurance, retirement plans, contingency cash reserves, fire protection, and endowment policies. Now minority carriers are moving into the traditionally closed activity of group policy underwriting.

In comparing minority carriers to other participants in the life insurance industry, we find that minorities have a higher level of representation than they

---

[g]The purpose of shifting from 1972 to an earlier year, 1969, was to compensate for data limitations. However, this should not affect the logical continuity of the analysis.

do in the other finance-related industries. In 1969 there were 1,787 companies in the insurance industry. Minority firms made up 10 percent of the group. Industry sales for this year were $172.8 billion overall, and total asset holding amounted to $197.2 billion. These aggregate figures indicate that the average gross receipts per firm in the industry were $96.7 million and per capita asset holdings were $110.4 million.

Although minority insurance companies have a larger numerical representation in the industry than is true in other finance-related industries, they nevertheless have a much smaller share of aggregate gross receipts. Minorities received 0.079 percent of the gross revenue generated by the industry. And if minority insurance companies' revenues continue to grow at 5 percent, we can expect the minority revenue share to increase to a full 1 percent by the turn of the century.

In terms of their asset holdings, this theme continues. Because of inadequate data, however, it is necessary to draw inferences from a limited sample. In August of 1970, the National Insurance Association (NIA), the nation's largest minority economic organization, held a national convention, which was attended by 43 minority-owned insurance companies. It was disclosed that these firms had assets totaling approximately $500 million. This indicates the average insurance company would have an asset structure of $11.6 million.

In making mean ratio comparisons between minority firms and the overall industry, we find that the average industry assets are 10 times as great. However, the disparity is probably greater when considering most minority firms, since it is safe to assume that the forty-three NIA affiliated companies were subsets of the smaller group of firms with annual receipts of one million dollars, rather than the 6.1 percent whose annual revenues were $23,000 per year.[h]

Market Imperfections

The tiny relative volume of minority firms' receipts and financial resources provides a partial explanation of why minority firms have a negligible impact on economic development. The one fact that is characteristic of all the finance-related industries, whether commercial banks and savings and loan associations, or mortgage bankers and insurance companies, is that they all have less than 1 percent of the available resources.

In the past financial institutions have in general, neglected minorities at large. Recently, a writer who was critical of Black banks did attest that, "Before the 1960s it was all but impossible for a Black to get an unsecured personal loan at a bank."[20] Similarly, another source cited that,

---

[h]The National Insurance Association and the Office of Minority Business Enterprise are jointly sponsoring management counseling and training programs for insurance company staffs to help them become more viable competitors in the industry and to diversify the types of service they offer businessmen and residents of low income communities. This may decrease the number of small scale marginal firms.

During hearings before a Senate Committee, it was revealed that only about 10 percent of Puerto Rican-American businesses had bank accounts; and only 5 percent used any type of bank credit.[21]

Conventional wisdom has argued that financial markets facilitate an exchange of claims, funds, or obligations, and that an optimum allocation of resources automatically takes place among all competing claims. But the question has not been raised as to whether all claims can compete equally, and how ownership and control influence the allocative mechanism. Are there different supply and demand subsidies among borrowers and lenders? Does one group of borrowers or investors have a greater degree of market power than another? Can a group of this type influence the flow of capital? The function of capital markets is to facilitate an exchange of funds between all savers and investors, and yet in practice we find that certain savers and investors are not on par with others, either socially or economically. There are those members of society that have varying degrees of market strength in terms of the knowledge and information they bring to a transaction, as well as wealth holding, purchasing power, and credit worthiness.

In minority communities, capital markets do not properly fulfill their functions; they do not provide minorities access to the U.S. aggregate flow of funds. The financial system does not generate financial instruments that are needed for underwriting economic development. The problem underlying this dysfunction is found in a rationing mechanism which affects both the available alternatives as well as the amount of financial resources. This rationing, which resembles rationing of foreign exchange, creates a distributive mechanism that penalizes minorities because of socioeconomic, intellectual, and cultural differences.

The existing system expresses definite social investment preferences which result from the previous allocation of income and which influence the allocation of resources for the present and future. The system compounds economic instability by perpetually increasing the inequality of income distribution. And, in the U.S. economy, a greater inequality of income distribution leads to a greater concentration in certain types of capital assets. A central problem of traditional financial market analysis is that most studies ignore financial markets' allocation deficiencies because of analysts' inherent preferences for the simple model of perfect competition. Conventional financial analysis pays limited attention to issues of market structure, dynamics, relative costs of information, and problems of income distribution. Market participants are viewed as being atomistic and homogeneous, and as having perfect foresight about capital market behavior. Also, it is assumed that each individual in the community at large has the same access to the market and opportunity to transact, and that each is socially and economically capable of expressing the preference that is appropriate to his individual interest. Moreover, it is assumed that transaction costs for providing or receiving various types of financial instruments are equally known and equally divided among all community members. As a result of this oversimplification, many critical questions are avoided.

There are various types of nonprice credit rationing that prevail in financial markets; price is not the sole criteria. Loan agreements between a financial institution and a borrower form a vector of contract terms which include interest rates and nonprice variables, such as compensating balances, credit standards, maturity restrictions, collateral and cosignee requirements, which establish old customer versus new customer preferences and local versus nonlocal customer preferences. Other nonprice variables are the public relations value of the individual customer, the use of the loan, the size and type of collateral, cosigner requirements, the value and type of the individual deposit, and the size of customer's initial deposit with the bank. Most of these practices have served to filter out the minority borrower.

Inelastic Demand

In examining the elements which affect the flow of capital into minority communities, we should begin by discussing the relationship between the rate of interest and the flow of funds per unit of time. In traditional circles, economists have generally posltulated that the flow of capital within a closed system is highly sensitive to interest rate changes. However, investigation of this relationship reveals that the rate of interest is not an important determinant of the flow of funds into the inner cities. A statistical survey of minority businessmen was conducted in which the businessmen were asked to list the factors that determined whether or not they received investment funds from lending institutions. Most respondents placed little emphasis upon the cost of borrowing, since they normally expected to pay higher rates of interest than borrowers outside the inner city, and since changes in the rate of interest did not affect the availability of capital. Also, most of the businessmen stated that their expected returns for a given venture were usually substantially above the negotiated rate of interest. The principal problem they identified was the acquisition of funds from financial institutions which were generally reluctant to make loans in the ghetto—not the level of interest rates.

Figure 1-1 shows graphically the type of minority community demand curve implied by these questionnaire results. The demand for loanable funds, either short-term, intermediate-, or long-term, is highly interest inelastic. This explains why there is little change in interest rates and money market conditions in minority communities; interest rates remain continuously high and funds remain scarce. The flow of funds and the amount of financial resources available to the communities are mainly supply determined. Demand can be treated as

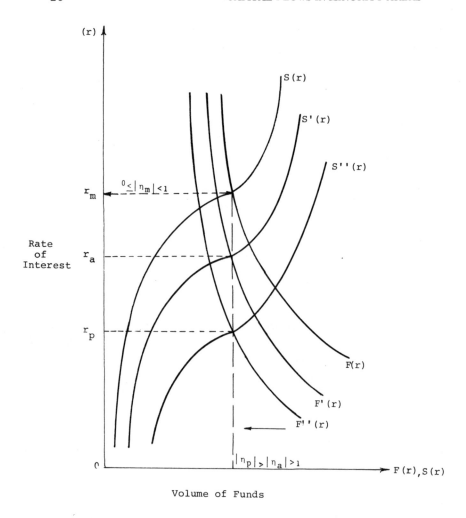

Figure 1-1. Various Loanable Funds Demand Functions.

given, and changes in the supply of funds and nonprice rationing practices are the variables that affect the financial conditions of the ghetto.

The demand for loanable funds in a minority community can probably be best described by a concave, discontinuous, kinked demand function. In Figure 1-1 we see a series of interest rates, r_p, r_a, and r_m, where r_p = the prime rate of interest that is charged to the largest and most desirable customers, r_a = the average interest rate charged nonprime borrowers, and r_m = the minority rate of interest. The arguments of the relationship are

$$\frac{\partial F}{\partial r_p} < \frac{\partial F}{\partial r_a} < \frac{\partial F}{\partial r_m} \leqslant 0$$

$$0 < |\eta_m| < 1 < |\eta_a| < |\eta_p| < +\infty$$

for their respective feasible domains. In Figure 1-1 we see that the loanable funds' demand function $F(r)$ has an inverse relationship with the rate of interest. For interest rates above r_m, minority firms are insensitive to changes in the cost of borrowing because of their excess demand for loanable funds. If alternative sources of capital were available, then demand adjustment would translate into elastic behavior. The demand for loanable funds would be incrementally affected only as long as the proportional change in the rate of interest is greater. The kinked demand shows that the effective demand for loanable funds is discontinuous beyond the minority interest threshold of r_m. There is a gap in the schedule and a discontinuous portion which depicts how minority firms would behave if they had access to alternative sources of funds. This is depicted by changes in the supply curve $S(r)$.

It is commonly stated that functional resources that have good substitutes have elastic demands. This, as Stigler noted, is a tautology. Substitution is defined in terms of the extent to which borrowers shift among alternative sources of capital when the relative costs change. Good substitutes therefore imply high demand elasticity. In the case of minorities, it is the lack of financial alternatives that adds to their demand inelasticity.

Partitioned Markets

Traditionally, and economy's financial system is viewed as containing F_j financial markets with R_j financial resources hosted in C_j communities ($j = 1$, $2, \ldots, n$) where $R_j \in F_j \in C_j$. Within each community, there exists an array of financial markets containing S_j and D_j individual supply and demand schedules, respectively, where at any given point in time $S_j - D_j = 0$, but in equilibrium

$$\sum_{j=1}^{n} S_j - \sum_{j=1}^{n} D_j = 0$$

In the aggregate treatment of a financial system, conventional wisdom views all participating units as independent, omniscient, homogeneous, and atomistic entities in the marketplace. Each demand and supply unit also behaves in a manner that gives it an additive property, which implies that the ratio between any element of supply or demand is always equal to unity:

$$\frac{S_1}{S_2} = \frac{S_3}{S_4} = \cdots = \frac{S_{n-1}}{S_n} = 1 \quad \text{and} \quad \frac{D_1}{D_2} = \frac{D_3}{D_4} = \cdots = \frac{D_{n-1}}{D_n} = 1$$

and in equilibrium

$$\sum_{j=1}^{n} \frac{S_{j-1}}{S_j} - \sum_{j=1}^{n} \frac{D_{j-1}}{D_j} = 0$$

In practice we observe the contrary, that is $S_{j-1}/S_j \lesseqgtr 1$ and/or $D_{j-1}/D_j \lesseqgtr 1$, as a result of existing externalities. In reality the financial system cannot be treated as a dichotomous division between a set of look-alike borrowers and lenders. Instead, we have a series of fragmented markets that are partitioned in accordance to varying degrees of market power and are not the consequence of public but rather of private collusive regulation. Within the S_jth and D_jth grouping, market power inequalities exist which have resulted in a compounding of resource inequality. The actual function and performance of the existing system is a perverted namesake from its purely competitive model in that it allocates and distributes financial resources to a limited number of users, assigns arbitrary and discretionary values to these resources, and provides growth and the capacity for economic change to the users in accordance to the power they can exercise in the marketplace.

The historic behavior of financial markets has resulted in a distribution of financial resources that has both micro and macro costs ramifications. In the U.S. economy, the inequality of resource distribution has resulted in financing of certain socially questionable types of tax avoidance assets, such as tax shelter walnut orchards, off-shore drilling sites, and mining exploration syndicates. Minority communities, in contrast, have not been able to afford the luxury of these types of investments, and instead are continuously faced with capital shortages. Financial capital is always thinly spread out over the limited selection of available assets.

Ultimately resource ownership and the prices paid for the uses of these resources affect income levels and income distribution. They influence a community's level of aggregate consumption and investment, its absorptive capacity for private and public capital formation, income diversification for reducing risks from economic cyclical fluctuations, and the social share of the output of goods and services.

The actual performance of the present financial system has resulted in a rightward skewed distribution of financial resources. There are many more individuals who receive much less than the average amount, than those who receive much more. This is especially true when we divide the population into ethnic minorities and nonminorities. To illustrate in notation how this has come about, let us say that p_i represents the cumulative percentage of households with resources less than m_i, and let us also allow for their cumulative percentage of aggregate resource holdings, q_i. Then, the Lorenz curve has its equation, $q_i = f(p_i)$. The resource holdings are divided into classes r_i, where r_i stands for the percentage of recipients in the resource class whose maximum resource holding is m_i. Then the area lying beneath the Lorenz curve is the sum of the areas of the series of polygons:

$$\frac{0+q_i}{2} \, r_i, \, \frac{q_i+q_2}{2} r_2, \ldots, \frac{q_n+q_{n-1}}{2} r_n$$

or in shorter form it can be expressed as $\frac{1}{2} \Sigma \, (q_j + q_{j-1}) r_j$.

Through the use of Lorenz curves and the rectangular distribution form, we can illustrate the inequality in financial resource distribution, assuming we have N resource holders who are equally spaced between values a and b. Then

$$p_i = \frac{1}{N} \int_a^t \frac{N}{b-a} \, dx = \frac{t-a}{b-a} \qquad q_i = \frac{\int_a^t \frac{N}{b-a} \, x \, dx}{\int_a^b \frac{N}{b-a} \, x \, dx} = \frac{t^2 - a^2}{b^2 - a^2}$$

If we eliminate the parameter t, we obtain the equation of the Lorenz curve:

$$q_i = \frac{p_i^2 \, (b-a) + 2ap_i}{b+a}$$

The area under the Lorenz curve would be

$$\int_0^1 q_i \, dp = \frac{b+2a}{3 \, (b+a)}$$

and since the line of equality is one-half the financial resource, inequality index I would be

$$I = \frac{\dfrac{1}{2} - \dfrac{b+2a}{3 \, (b+a)}}{\dfrac{1}{2}} = \frac{b-a}{3 \, (b+a)} \geqslant 0$$

for all nonnegative resource holdings. And if b is unity, then in the limit as $a \to 0$, $I = 1/3$, or in the limit as $a \to 1$, $I = 0$, which represents the range in moving from inequality towards complete equality. In a perfectly competitive financial system we would expect that

$$\frac{S_{j-1}}{S_j} = \frac{D_{j-1}}{D_j} = 1 = b \to \lim_{a \to 0} I = 0$$

However the point in fact is that we observe market power inequalities both on the demand and supply side and the consequence is that it is always true that

$$\frac{S_{j-1}}{S_j} \lessgtr 1, \quad \frac{D_{j-1}}{D_j} \lessgtr 1 \Rightarrow I > 0$$

The social consequence of this type of financial system is that the allocative mechanism systematically perpetuates a less than optimal situation for minority communities, not only in terms of the variety of financial capital sources, but also in terms of the level of resource allocation. Due to the heterogeneity in market power that prevails in the existing system, arbitrary market and non-market values can be assigned which impose discriminatory barriers, preventing access to the standard vehicles of finance. These walls of discrimination have prevented the allocation mechanism from functioning properly, have fragmented and isolated minority financial markets, and have perpetuated chronic excess demand.

In summary, the salient features of financial markets in minority communities are as follows. Markets are partitioned and function as separate subsystems of major financial centers. Financial markets operate properly when they are purely competitive and neither borrowers nor lenders possess a competitive edge in the market. However, since these conditions do not prevail in practice, financial markets are always operating at less than socially optimal conditions. Distribution of financial resources is severely rationed both in the aggregate amount and on a per capita basis. Due to the continuous limited allocation of funds, minority communities have a modest capital endowment for creating conditions conducive to economic change and development.

2
Credit and Credit Markets in the Inner Cities

Credit and Consumption

In most of the introductory literature on the microeconomic behavior of the household, discussion of the use or the rationale for consumer credit is absent or superficial. The purpose of this chapter is therefore to explore the role of consumer credit and credit market performance.

In the typical classical setting, households are viewed as being confronted with a set of alternative choices between goods and services that must be exercised within a given income constraint. Households are seen as being capable of clearly defining their preferences and of being well-informed about the schedule of relative prices. Given this information, and assuming that income and the relative prices of alternatives remain constant, one can easily derive from a cluster of indifference curves an inverse demand curve of any individual good by varying the price of that good. Of course, one must allow for the various properties of convexity, divisibility, and the absence of external diseconomies. Considering the limited dimensions of this discussion, it is understandable that the notion of credit is not incorporated into traditional analysis.

It is as though a barter exchange were taking place between economic units—an automatic frictionless exchange of inputs and outputs, with households having at all times the inherent opportunity to exchange. Consumers always have sufficient purchasing power to clear their basic market needs. Members of the household are not considered vulnerable to involuntary or structural unemployment, nor are they viewed as wishing out of necessity to consume beyond their current income level in order to maintain a reasonable level of consumption. To borrow for the pure sake of consumption is not in conventional analysis considered a rational decision.

Actually it is not unreasonable to expect that a household, even if fully employed, would still turn to the use of credit for consumption ends. This is the case for most consumers since households' consumption preferences over time often do not coincide with their current pecuniary capacity to transact. Households frequently wish to consume now at the expense of borrowing against tomorrow's income. This is particularly true for purchases, such as automobiles, washing machines, stoves, refrigerators, or any other number of durables. Most of these purchases are not transacted on a cash basis.

National income analysts, when developing their aggregate social accounts, have chosen to treat residential housing purchases as a form of capital formation

25

because of the continuous services they render. This implies that mortgage financing is rational since households are concerned with acquiring a physical asset rather than a consumption good.

Others view housing as a financial asset. For those households which expect at some time in the future to capitalize from the appreciation of property values or to earn income or tax advantages from subletting their dwellings, this may be a justifiable classification. However, some members of society who cannot realize nor visualize returns from rents or capital gains, view the mortgage financing of a dwelling as a pure consumption expenditure. In order to purchase a home, most families have to borrow against future earnings and repay debt as they continue to consume the service, with zero expectation of future returns.

Low income families make many purchases other than durables which have to be financed on a buy-now-pay-later basis. In minority communities it is not uncommon to encounter families having to finance the basic essentials, such as food and clothing, through the use of credit. Fortunately, these credit transactions at times have reciprocal benefits. For example, if it were not for credit sales, small retail outlets such as "mom and pop's" grocery stores would be unable to operate and would quickly become insolvent. Many of their sales can only be transacted on an informal credit basis that involves no formal applications or credit screening. The criterion for extending credit is the frequency at which a person patronizes one of these outlets. In most instances, credit is extended to low income families without interest charges. This arrangement works to the advantage of inner city residents who would have to reduce their levels of subsistence if they could not purchase their basic necessities on credit.

As a consequence of inadequate income, minorities are forced to seek financing for most of their consumption expenditures, whether they involve durables, nondurables, or perishables. To imagine that consumer credit financing for the poor is an exercise of time preference or marginal trade-offs is to assume that an individual consumes during the current period because he plans or is willing to consume less in the future. Actually, it is a question of present survival; the future is deemed remote and not a relevant consideration. People living in poverty do not consider the future worth contemplating, but mentally block it out and only concern themselves with their present need to survive. Their view is similar to the Keynesian adage that in the long run we will all be dead; the poor visualize a shorter long-run horizon. Therefore, the extensive use of credit by minorities cannot be interpreted as demonstrating a stronger preference for current consumption; many of their credit purchases evolve out of basic necessity, rather than from intertemporal consumption trade-offs.

Credit and Poverty

In the inner cities, credit plays a vital role at all levels of consumption, although in some respects, the importance of credit is similar for the poor and the average consumer. There are, however, certain distinct differences, particularly in the availability of alternative sources and in prevailing terms. As a commissioner for the Federal Trade Commission stated at the American Industrial Bankers Association Second Annual Public Affairs Conference,

> Consumer credit has become a vitally important part of our economy. Today for many middle-income consumers the ready availability of credit for almost every type of product or service has enabled them to enjoy a standard of living never before conceived of in past decades.
>
> Yet for the low-income consumer for whom credit is not a matter of choice but one of vital necessity normal sources of credit are not generally available. Thus, low-income consumers are almost totally dependent today either on the ghetto merchant, the neighborhood finance company or the loan shark for the credit which they so desperately need in order to fill their simplest and most basic needs. The result of this dependence is that in the midst of our new found affluence, the persons who most need the credit are paying the highest price for it.[1]

If minorities are being exploited by nonminority creditors, then one wonders why they have not established their own credit institutions to challenge the domination of credit by nonminorities. One researcher who examined ethnic business participation found that differences in minorities' ability to compete in the business sphere largely depended on whether their credit institutions were able to survive the strains of emigration. Asian American institutions were seen as able to survive, whereas similar Black institutions, as well as family structure, were viewed as destroyed during Black enslavement.[2]

The issue that emerges is why is the distribution of credit and its related constraints different in the inner cities. The subject needs attention because it relates to low income groups' ability to increase their purchasing power beyond their current income. In examining the issue, we see that credit constraints apply relatively greater pressures on minorities because of their greater burden of poverty. It is generally understood that a reference to poverty in the urban centers pertains to the ethnic minority segment of society. As one researcher investigating the financing of the inner cities stated:

> With a number of measures now before Congress, there has been no let up in the debate over the problem of the "inner city"—a term which, in its human dimensions, increasingly has become synonymous with all the problems of minority groups in the nation's population. At all levels—national, state, and local—and in both the public and private sectors . . . high rates of unemployment and underemployment, attendant low levels of income, inadequate housing, rising crime rates, a flight of capital and eroding tax base, and a deteriorating social overhead (schools, hospitals, transportation facilities, and the like).[3]

Another author stated that:

> On the basis of the 1968 Social Security Administration definition of
> poverty there were 12.9 million poor people in metropolitan areas
> during that year. Of the total, 67 percent, or 8.6 million, were white;
> the remaining 4.3 million were nonwhites. This, of course, means that
> urban poverty is absolutely a greater problem for white people. How-
> ever, relatively it is a greater problem for Blacks, since Blacks comprised
> 16.8 percent of the total population of urban areas, but about 30 per-
> cent of the urban poor (in 1970). Moreover, in central cities of metro-
> politan areas, nonwhite people comprised an even greater proportion
> of the poor. This figure indicates that the closer one gets to the center
> or 'downtown' of the typical urban area, the more likely one is to find
> poor, Black people.[4]

And this may not change in the future since it is estimated that:

> By 1985, too, probably 90 percent or more of the non-white popula-
> tion will still reside in metropolitan areas—a 150 percent increase in
> actual numbers—and most of that increase will continue to take place
> in the inner cities, with all their problems of unemployment, low
> income, and substandard housing.[5]

However, it is also likely that Chicanos will be found as one approaches the
urban center, since in 1970 the Bureau of the Census showed that less than 10
percent of the Chicano population resided in rural areas, with most residing in
urban areas.

The tragedy of poverty among these members of society might well have
been extracted from a play by Sophocles, in that the socioeconomic sins of the
head of the household are passed on to the offspring. Consequently, poverty
inevitably continues to perpetuate itself and remains unchanged by the overall
economic progress of others. Thus, the poverty among minorities is characterized by a cycle of perpetuity. The elements that reinforce this perpetuation of
poverty are illustrated in Figure 2–1, which shows the chain of events that adds
to the socioeconomic problems of minorities. Because of this continuous
poverty cycle, sincere efforts aimed at ameliorating conditions for the poor must
involve a more than even-handed treatment of minorities by credit markets, in
order to offset other imposing constraints.

Minority wage earners are typically in low income occupations. They are
also subject to more frequent and longer periods of unemployment. As described
in the parlance of the ghetto, minorities are treated as an accounting adjustment
similar to the practice of LIFO—Last In, First Out.

These manpower problems force employed members of the inner cities to
dissave and draw down their financial assets. Providing credit for the unemployed
thus becomes more necessary and, at the same time, more difficult. Inner city

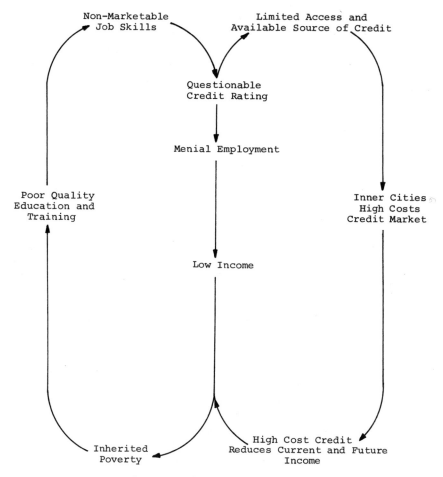

Figure 2-1. Minority Poverty Cycle.

residents for the most part do not have equal access to credit markets because of the misconceptions others may have about them, or the lack of information that they have about credit markets, which prevents them from receiving credit.

Members of the minority community are often classified as submarginal credit risks, without knowing why they were rejected or what constitutes an appropriate credit rating. Many of the social attributes necessary for establishing credit are the qualities which minorities do not possess or are still developing.

Minorities are considered to have a submarginal credit status because they are viewed as falling below the margin of acceptable risk. This status and the resulting inability to acquire credit are attributable to several factors—the type of employment, length of employment tenure, and an income threshold that is considered insufficient to service a debt. Other reasons for which minorities may be refused credit are lack of established credit references (references outside of the inner city having a premium rating), previous loss of credit, and questionable credit record in the past. The latter two conditions may be a permanent detriment to credit establishment, even though at some point in the future the individual may have a more stable source or higher level of income. Other credit rating factors associated with credit worthiness are owning a home, maintaining permanent residency at the same address for a number of years, having a telephone, not having been divorced, being a nonminority male above or below certain ages, having clear title to a relatively new automobile with sufficient blue book recovery value, a reasonable savings account, a paid life insurance policy, or an adequate portfolio of marketable securities.[6] Many of these screening criteria cancel the hopes of inner city residents for obtaining credit.

In addition to minorities' difficulty in meeting these credit criteria, other explanations are frequently offered for the limited credit available to minorities. One rather dubious argument is that for public relations reasons the typical nonminority financial institution might find it more difficult to charge minorities as high a rate as some minority-owned or interracial banks charge for their consumer loans, so they avoid lending to minorities. Another common argument is that private lending institutions are simply not structured to take high risks since they are lending "other people's money" and must be concerned with and limit the volume of high risk loans they extend. Also, the concern about increases in debt at many levels throughout the nation may further restrict the flow of credit to inner cities because of lenders' fear of the social opprobrium which they might incur if they were forced to foreclose or take legal recourse against minority borrowers who entered default. These arguments that have been offered are at best rationalizations aimed at justifying the current status quo.

Inner city residents find it especially difficult to acquire mortgage credit for the purchase of a home. Not only are mortgage funds extremely scarce, but the cost of borrowing and credit restrictions prevent many inner cities residents from having equal access to the market. Because the amount of funds necessary for the purchase of a dwelling is much more than for a typical consumer purchase, more evidence is required regarding permanency and stability of employment, regularity of income, and availability of sufficient capital for the initial down payment.

Recently, the Bureau of Labor Statistics, in its studies of *Three Standards of Living for an Urban Family of Four Persons, 1969–1970,* disclosed that housing expenditures usually amount to 25 percent of income. This means that households with incomes of $9,560 or less cannot afford a $20,000, 30-year mortgage carrying an effective interest rate of 7½ percent. According to *Social Indicators, 1973,* this cost of mortgage financing would imply that approximately 75 percent of the minority families were priced out of the housing market, since their income levels were below this amount. In 1975, mortgage rates escalated to above 9 percent. This would indicate that during this period more than 81 percent of the minority households were priced out of the market.[a]

The private business sector has not been without help from the public in that:

> Even when private lenders have been willing to make mortgage loans in high risk ghetto areas, the government itself (under Congressional mandate) has until recently pursued a policy of "redlining" economically depressed areas.[7]

Further, minority firms have found it difficult to acquire credit for expansion of new businesses. The reasons given are lack of collateral, insufficient business experience in handling business loan applications, and the necessity of operating in inner cities' small-scale markets. The outflow of capital from the inner cities can be explained in part by lenders' expectation of making less risky and more profitable investments elsewhere. Also, the lower taxes in suburbs can often attract funds away from the inner cities where higher taxes generally prevail. Similarly, slum properties do not attract funds for improvements because local tax laws penalize property improvements and because the federal income tax laws provide an allowance for rapid depreciation; the older and more dilapidated the structure, the more rapidly the depreciation allowance grows. This prevents financial resources from being allocated towards the physical improvement needs of the inner cities, and adds additional obstacles to home ownership.

Some observers would identify the lack of credit availability as one of the single most pressing problems that confronts minorities. However, availability is only part of the problem since the costs of credit, and other terms that are prerequisite to acquiring credit, limit an applicant's access to this form of financing. To equate availability with access is to think that neighboring supply is the same as actual supply. If this were true, then we would expect the neighboring residents of Fort Knox to reap pecuniary benefits from their proximity to the U.S. Government gold cache.

Nevertheless, in viewing credit availability in the inner cities, we see that it has been rationed by financial institutions to the extent that it has become necessary for inner city residents to turn to "gougers" and "loan sharks" to meet their credit needs. As Senator Proxmire attested before the Financial Institutions Subcommittee of the Banking and Currency Committee:

> The problem of obtaining adequate consumer credit in the ghetto on reasonable terms is becoming of national concern. A recent report by the Kerner Commission listed consumer exploitation of ghetto residents as one of the chief causes of urban riots . . . the 7 years of records of hearings on truth in lending point to one inescapable conclusion and

---

[a]Actually, it was as early as March 1970 when the American Bankers disclosed that the Bank of America was charging 9 to 9¼ percent on conventional mortgages.

that is that the poor pay more. However, many of us simply have not realized just how much more the poor actually do pay until the release of an excellent study by the Federal Trade Commission. Although the study was confined to the District of Columbia, I believe the conditions here are broadly representative of credit practices throughout the Nation.[8]

David Caplovitz in *The Poor Pay More: Consumer Practices of Low-Income Families,* a study which surveyed the slums of Harlem in New York City, came up with a similar conclusion to Senator Proxmire's, that no matter how you look at it, minorities pay more. Some individuals might argue that the Truth In Lending Act has corrected this problem. However, this legislation does not prevent retailers from adding credit charges to the purchase price of a product. Some inner city retailers treat all credit costs by including them in the price. Disclosure of finance charges, in this case, has had little impact in correcting the problem of high credit charges in the ghetto.

One of the justifications given for the existence of higher credit costs in the ghetto is that conducting business in the inner city is a hazardous and risky business; hence, it is only reasonable to expect that credit costs would be higher. However, as Congressional hearings disclosed, only a quarter of the additional costs can be attributed to credit losses, and the remaining three-quarters are a result of inefficient or costly selling practices on the part of the inner cities merchants, due to their reliance on the antiquated, hard sell methods of door-to-door selling. Higher prices are also due to the lack of product price competition in the inner city. The merchants often substitute credit competition for price and quality competition.

Minority area merchants' advertising usually emphasizes their policy of granting credit even to the most unpromising customers. Some merchants will actually stress the fact that they will extend credit even though others have refused, or even though the customer may have a poor credit rating. This willingness on the part of the ghetto merchants to extend "easy credit" permits them to sell at substantially higher prices and to impose greater credit charges. Ghetto residents, because of their low income level, discounted credit rating, and consequent inability to obtain credit from sources that are accessible to the average nonminority American, have no recourse but to pay greater credit charges and higher prices for their goods and services. They must often behave as "captive buyers" in the sense that they have limited options to transact elsewhere.

Some would argue that credit is a scarce resource and ghetto residents should not expect to be treated differently from people in the suburbs. Rightfully, there is a sizeable segment in the ghetto that should not receive credit just as there is an equivalent group in the suburbs that should not receive credit. However, the problem is that the minority subset not receiving credit continues to be a larger comparative segment of the universe.

Residents of the inner cities have simply not been able to enjoy direct credit sources, such as commercial banks, savings and loans, or other established financial institutions. The reason generally offered to explain this situation is that minorities' modest and unstable levels of income raise doubt about their financial ability to service and repay debts. This explanation implies the assumption that income levels can accurately reflect capacity to retire a given debt. This may be true if what we are measuring and equating are two stocks, a stock of purchasing power income (Is) and the stock of claims debt (Ds). However, the truth of the matter is that we are comparing not stocks but flows. The given flow of debt dDs/dt needs to be compared to the household's flow of income dIs/dt over a forecasted period of time to determine if $dIs/dt - dDs/dt$ is less than, equal to, or greater than zero.

If a credit transaction involves a perishable or a nondurable, it is generally true that most purchases will amount to only a fraction of the consumer's income, $0 < Ds/Is < 1$. On the other hand, in the credit transactions of certain types of durables, such as housing, automobiles, and so on, the credit purchase to income ratio is often expected to be greater than unity. Few houses would be purchased if credit or income ratios were expected to be $Ds/Is \leq 1$.

In the case of both durable and nondurable credit purchases, it is not evident that credit institutions adhere to some catholic rule of thumb either to determine an appropriate measure of debt to income, which would warrant the extension or rejection of credit, or to develop their schedule of probabilities for forecasting expected income flow. It is apparent that creditors make their income projections and determine an optimum balance by intuition and small sample testing. Unfortunately, these practices are not uniformly applied to all borrowers since the forecast becomes less conservative and debt to income ratio requirements become less rigorous the more removed an individual is from the minority community.

Minority Credit Institutions

In 1969 minority-owned credit institutions accounted for $25 million of the industry's receipts. Employee-type firms received 99 percent of the total revenue. When compared to Transamerica Financial Corporation, which ranked twentieth in revenue among diversified financial companies, we see that the total receipts of minority credit institutions only amounted to a little over 1 percent. In comparing minority receipts to the fifty largest diversified financial companies, we see that their percentage share of total revenue dropped to six-hundredth of 1 percent, even though they represented 6 percent of the number of firms within the credit industry.

Inequalities in revenue are not solely limited to comparisons between minor-

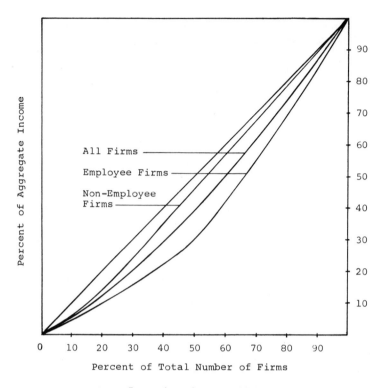

Figure 2-2. Revenue Inequalities between Minority Nonbank Credit Institutions. Source: *Minority-Owned Businesses: 1969,* MB-1, Bureau of the Census, Department of Commerce, August 1971.

ity and nonminority firms, but are also discernible between minority credit agencies in general, and employee and non-employee-type firms, as seen in Figure 2-2. Revenue disparities are also observable between various ethnic groups, with Spanish-speaking and other minorities showing the greatest inequalities. These conditions are illustrated in Figure 2-3.

Credit agencies identified as "not specifically known" by the Bureau of the Census survey of *Minority-Owned Business: 1969,* disclosed that they accounted for two-thirds of the receipts. Their annual revenue was 17 million dollars. Consumer credit companies were second in annual gross receipts. In 1969 their revenue volume was $7 million. These two industries also show the highest per capita figures—$130,000 for "not specifically known" credit agencies and $89,000 for personal credit companies. These are also the two industries with the greatest employment levels. Business credit agencies and loan correspondents accounted for 5 percent of the volume. They averaged $2,000 in annual receipts, indicating that only a modest source of funds can be provided to the minority business community by its indigenous lending institutions.

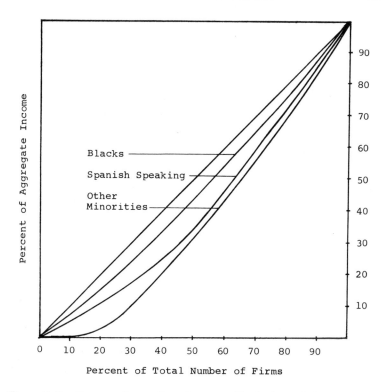

Figure 2-3. Revenue Inequalities between Black, Spanish-Speaking, and Other Minority Nonbank Credit Institutions. Source: *Minority-Owned Businesses: 1969,* MB-1, Bureau of the Census, Department of Commerce, August 1971.

Most of the credit institutions mentioned could not be readily identified by the Bureau's survey, so it is possible there may be some business financing that is not detectable by the data from those credit agencies we can identify. The evidence indicates that most financing is provided to minority consumers, which would serve to indicate why few, if any, inner city funds are available for financing capital formation.

The size and distribution of revenue, the number of firms and employment levels can be seen in Tables 2-1 and 2-2. The ranking of importance in terms of the volume of receipts is virtually the same for employee and non-employee-type firms. This shows that there is very little difference in the prominence of one industry over another, even though there may be scale differences in size, both in terms of their volume and their employment levels. In 1969, there were 235 minority credit companies. Sixty-five percent of these were employee-type firms with an average of 5 employees per firm and average receipts of $164,493 annually. Although non-employee-type firms constituted 35 percent of the

Table 2-1
Size and Distribution of Revenues for Minority Credit Companies, 1969

Firm Category / Industry Classification	Gross and Average Receipts in Thousands of Dollars					
	All		Employee-Type		Non-Employee Type	
	Gross	Average Receipts per Firm	Gross	Average Receipts per Firm	Gross	Average Receipts per Firm
All Credit Agencies	25,467	108.4	25,003	164.5	464	5.6
Personal	6,960	89.2	6,895	102.9	65	5.9
Business	1,186	74.1	1,166	129.56	20	2.2
Loan Correspondent	230	23.0	217	36.2	13	4.2
Credit not specifically known	17,091	130.5	16,725	238.83	366	6.0
All Credit Agencies						
Percentage of All Credit	100.0		98.2		1.8	
Personal						
Percentage of All Credit	27.3		27.6		14.0	
Percentage of Industry	100.0		99.1		0.8	
Business						
Percentage of All Credit	4.7		4.7		4.3	
Percentage of Industry	100.0		98.3		1.7	
Loan Correspondent						
Percentage of All Credit	0.9		0.9		2.8	
Percentage of Industry	100.0		94.3		5.7	
Credit not specifically known						
Percentage of All Credit	67.1		66.9		78.9	
Percentage of Industry	100.0		97.9		2.1	

Source: *Minority-Owned Businesses: 1969*, MB-1, Bureau of the Census, Department of Commerce, August 1971.

Table 2-2
Employment Characteristics of Minority Finance Companies, 1969

Firm Category / Industry Classification	All	Number of Firms and Employees				Non-Employee-Type
	Number of Employees	Employee-Type				
		Number of Firms	Average Number of Employees	Average Revenue Product (In Thousands of Dollars)		
All Credit Agencies	235	817	152	5	30.6	83
Personal	78	391	67	6	17.6	11
Business	16	52	9	6	22.4	7
Loan Correspondent	10	11	6	2	19.7	4
Credit not specifically known	131	363	70	5	46.1	61
All Credit Agencies						
Percentage of All Credit	100.0		64.7			35.3
Personal						
Percentage of All Credit	33.0		44.1			13.3
Percentage of Industry	100.0		85.9			14.1
Business						
Percentage of All Credit	7.0		5.9			8.4
Percentage of Industry	100.0		56.3			43.7
Loan Correspondent						
Percentage of All Credit	4.0		3.9			4.8
Percentage of Industry	100.0		60.0			40.0
Credit not specifically known						
Percentage of All Credit	56.0		46.1			73.5
Percentage of Industry	100.0		53.4			46.6

Source: *Minority-Owned Businesses: 1969*, MB-1, Bureau of the Census, Department of Commerce, August 1971.

number of minority credit companies, they received less than 1 percent of the gross revenues.

In Tables 2–3 through 2–5, a general distribution is presented of the receipts, number of firms, and employees. Black-owned credit companies generated the largest volume of gross receipts. They accounted for 50 percent of the revenue and represented 47 percent of the minority firms. Sixty-nine percent of the Black credit companies fell into the "not specifically known" category and they produced three-fourths of the revenue. Personal finance companies were the second major source of credit for the Black community. Business credit companies and loan correspondent firms were relatively unimportant. Black firms also accounted for almost half of the employees in the inner city credit industry.

The Spanish-speaking represented 39 percent of the minority credit companies and received only 9 percent of the receipts generated by minority credit companies. There were two-and-a-half times as many Spanish-speaking firms as other minorities; nevertheless, other minorities' market share of receipts was four times as great as the Spanish-speaking share.

Spanish-speaking industry representation differed from the other two ethnic groups in that the major share of receipts originated in personal consumer finance. This industry also hosted the largest number of Spanish-speaking firms. The one trait that seemed to prevail among all three ethnic groups was their relatively weak position in the business credit field.

Institutional Sources of Credit

The major institutional sources of credit located in the inner cities are commercial banks, finance companies, credit unions, mutual savings banks, and savings and loan associations. These institutions in the past have shown little interest in providing credit to inner cities residents, and have made available only a small volume of funds to these residents in comparison to the credit extended to the community of large corporations. Indeed, the large corporations remain in command of most of the financing, by virtue of both the loan commitments made to them from interlocking directorships and their ability to out-maneuver smaller borrowers in financial negotiations.

In the case of commercial banks, a recent quarterly survey by the congressional staff of the Subcommittee on Domestic Finance, Committee on Banking and Currency found that in general, a very small proportion of the business loans made by commercial banks is directed to small firms at any interest rate, prime or higher.

> To gauge the performance of commercial banks in extending credit to small business borrowers, Arthur Burns, Chairman of the Committee on Interest and Dividends, stated, "there is a correlation between size of loan and size of borrowers [and] the data from this survey for the two

Table 2-3
Interethnic Revenue Shares for Minority Credit Firms, 1969

| | Gross Receipts in Thousands of Dollars | | | | | |
| | Black | | Spanish-Speaking | | Other Minorities | |
	Gross	Percent	Gross	Percent	Gross	Percent
All Credit Agencies	12,644	49.6	2,280	9.0	10,543	41.4
Personal Credit	2,242	32.2	1,512	21.7	3,206	46.1
Interethnic in Percent	17.7		66.3		30.4	
Business Credit			6	0.5		
Interethnic in Percent			0.3			
	(917)	(64.7)	(140)	(9.8)	(359)	(25.4)
	(7.3)		(6.1)		(3.4)	
Loan Correspondent			134			
Interethnic in Percent						
Credit Agencies	9,485	55.0	628	3.7	6,978	40.8
(not specifically known)	75.0		27.5		66.2	

Source: *Minority-Owned Businesses: 1969*, MB-1, Bureau of the Census, Department of Commerce, August 1971.

smallest loan size categories—$1,000–$9,999 and $10,000–$99,999—are indicative of the volume of new lending at the prime rate to smaller businesses.[9]

Short-term business loans totaled $3,452,841,000, according to the quarterly survey for February 1973. Loans to small businesses constituted only $51.6 million of this amount, and this was disbursed in loans of less than $100,000.

Table 2-4
Composition of Industry Participation among Minority Credit Companies

| | Number of Firms | | | | | |
| | Black | | Spanish-Speaking | | Other Minorities | |
	Number	Percent	Number	Percent	Number	Percent
All Credit Agencies	111	47.0	91	39.0	33	14.0
Personal Credit	25	32.1	43	55.1	10	12.8
Interethnic in Percent	23.0		18.3		30.3	
Business Credit	7	43.8	3	18.8	6	37.5
Interethnic in Percent	6.0		3.3		18.2	
Loan Correspondent	2	20.0	7	70.0	1	10.0
Interethnic in Percent	2.0		7.7		3.0	
Credit Agencies	77	58.8	38	29.0	16	12.2
(not specifically known)	69.0		41.8		48.5	

Source: *Minority-Owned Businesses: 1969*, MB-1, Bureau of the Census, Department of Commerce, August 1971.

Table 2-5
Employment Levels among Black, Spanish-Speaking, and Other Minorities
Finance Companies, 1969

	Number of Employees					
	Black		Spanish-Speaking		Other Minorities	
	Number	Percent	Number	Percent	Number	Percent
All Credit Agencies	393	48.1	120	14.7	304	37.2
Personal Credit					159	40.7
Interethnic in Percent					52.3	
Business Credit	(183)	(33.5)	(103)	(22.7)		
Interethnic in Percent	(47.1)		(85.8)		(7)	(11.1)
Loan Correspondent					(2.3)	
Interethnic in Percent						
Credit Agencies	208	57.3	17	4.7	138	38.0
(not specifically known)	71.0		14.2		45.4	

Source: *Minority-Owned Businesses: 1969*, MB-1, Bureau of the Census, Department of Commerce, August 1971.

Loans of more than $100,000 totaled $3,401,159,000; these were presumably made to large firms. Thus, only 1.5 percent, out of the total of nearly $3.5 billion in short-term loans, went to small businesses.

A similar bias towards large businesses is evident in revolving and long-term loans. When we add all these loan categories' totals together, we see that borrowers in the two smallest categories received only 1.8 percent, or $86,921,000 of the $4,416,339,000 total. Thus, minorities face a double burden. One is based on their ethnic origin; the other is based on the fact that they are still infants in a financial world of large adults.

The same situation is evident in the amount of bank credit available to finance companies, which historically has been the major institutional source of credit for minorities. For finance companies the alternative source available is the commercial paper market, which is equally dominated by the large corporations. This is especially true during periods of tight credit conditions. The consequence is that during these periods of aggregate credit scarcity, credit options are virtually eliminated for the inner cities, and their economic cyclical downturn is much more pronounced.

In 1972 the Federal Reserve disclosed that consumer credit totaled $127 billion. This amounted to almost $1,700 per household. The corresponding expenditures varied from home repairs, personal loans, and charge accounts to a wide variety of other purchases. Of the competing sources of credit, commercial banks and finance companies were the most dominant, as can be discerned from the ranking of values and the geometric means in Tables 2-6 and 2-7.

Finance companies are not only an important source of credit for the inner

Table 2-6
The Various Sources of Installment Credit (Amounts Supplied in Millions
of Dollars

| End of Period | Total | Financial Institutions | | | |
		Commercial Banks	Finance Companies[a]	Credit Unions	Miscellaneous Lenders
1940	$ 5,514	$ 1,452	$ 2,278	$ 171	$ 17
1945	2,462	745	910	102	19
1950	14,703	5,798	5,315	590	102
1955	28,906	10,601	11,838	1,678	281
1960	42,968	16,672	15,435	3,923	643
1965	70,893	28,962	23,851	7,324	965
1966	76,245	31,319	24,796	8,255	1,060
1967	79,428	33,152	24,576	9,003	1,213
1968	87,745	37,936	26,074	10,300	1,417
1969	97,105	42,421	27,846	12,028	1,694
1970	102,064	45,398	27,678	12,986	2,102
1971	111,295	51,240	28,883	14,770	2,251
1972	127,332	59,783	32,088	16,913	2,598

[a]Finance companies consist of those institutions formerly classified as sales finance, consumer finance, and other finance companies. Miscellaneous lenders include savings and loan associations and mutual savings banks. Note financial institution columns will not add up to the total column because this is the sum total from all sources which includes categories not cited.

Source: *Financial Institutions: Reform and the Public Interest*, op. cit., p. 125.

city, but an important line of credit for the nation. In 1972 finance companies provided 25.2 percent of all installment credit. If consumer installment credit supplied by finance companies, which totaled $32 billion, is added to $26.1 billion for business credit, we have a total of $58.1 billion in financing that was produced by this group.

Unfortunately, the market shares in terms of the volume of loans are very unevenly distributed among the firms within the industry. The Consumer Finance Association estimates there were between 4,000 and 5,000 finance companies in the year 1972. The one hundred largest firms, which constituted between 2 and 2.5 percent of the industry, accounted for 99.5 percent of all credit extended by these institutions.[10] Of these 100 finance companies, the ten largest had loan portfolios totaling $35 billion in 1972, which accounted for 60 percent of all credit extended. The top 20 firms loaned a total of $44.1 billion, which accounted for 76.19 percent of the finance company loan volume. (Table 2-8 shows this skewed distribution and lists the firms that make up this controlling group.) The consequence is that the finance company industry, a crucial source of consumer credit in the U.S., is dominated by a handful of firms which constitute less than 1 percent of the total number of firms in the industry.

The concentration of economic power among a few financial titans will become more pronounced in the future if the present trend towards acquisition

Table 2-7
Proportional Ranking of the Various Sources of Installment Credit

	Financial Institutions			
End of Period	Finance Companies	Commercial Banks	Credit Unions	Miscellaneous Lenders
1940	41.31	26.33	3.10	0.31
1945	36.96	30.26	4.87	0.77
1950	36.15	39.43	4.01	0.69
1955	40.95	36.67	5.80	0.97
1960	35.92	38.80	9.13	1.50
1965	33.64	40.85	10.33	1.36
1966	32.52	41.08	10.82	1.39
1967	30.94	41.74	11.33	1.53
1968	29.72	43.23	11.73	1.61
1969	28.68	43.69	12.39	1.74
1970	27.12	44.48	12.72	2.06
1971	25.95	46.04	13.27	2.02
1972	25.20	46.95	13.28	2.04
Geometric Mean	34.01	39.49	8.56	1.24

Source: *Financial Institutions: Reform and the Public Interest*, Staff Report of the Sub-committee in Domestic Finance, Committee on Banking and Currency, House of Representatives, August 1973, p. 125.

continues among bank holding companies. This will make it even more difficult for minority lending institutions to develop beyond the confines of the ghetto boundaries.

Federal government regulation of finance companies could be helpful in controlling this concentration of economic power and in improving conditions for minority borrowers. Aside from the Truth in Lending provisions of the Consumer Protection Act, the regulation of the performance of finance companies has remained relatively neglected by the federal government. Historically, the government has relegated borrowers to a back seat position and has emphasized the protection of depositors and the maintenance of financially sound lending institutions. The recent proposals offered by the Federal Reserve Board and the Hunt Commission have not varied considerably from this traditional stance. Most of the recommendations are aimed at safeguarding the borrower and the liquidity of the lender, rather than at providing proposed regulations for ensuring an adequate supply of credit at reasonable rates of interest for the economically disenfranchised.

One observer, in his recent assessment of the effect of the Hunt Commission recommendations on the inner cities, stated that:

The Commission failed to recognize the over-riding social and economic deficiency in the U.S., the economic disparity between the non-

Table 2-8

The Twenty Largest Finance Companies: Market Share of Loans in the
United States (by Loan Volume Size in Thousands of Dollars for
Dec. 31, 1972)

Finance Company	Loan Volume	Percentage Total	Cumulative Percentage
General Motors Acceptance Corp., New York, N.Y.	11,766,337	20.30	20.30
Ford Motor Credit Company, Dearborn, Mich.	5,230,900	9.00	29.30
Commerical Credit Company, Baltimore. Md.	3,210,690	5.53	34.83
Sears Roebuck Acceptance Corp., Wilmington, Del.	2,660,900	4.58	39.41
General Electric Credit Corp., New York, N.Y.	2,648,319	4.56	43.97
CIT Financial Corp., New York, N.Y.	2,566,298	4.42	48.39
Chrysler Financial Corp., Southfield, Mich.	1,972,819	3.40	51.79
Household Finance Corp., Chicago, Ill.	1,879,490	3.23	55.02
Associate Corp. of North American, New York, N.Y.	1,655,813	2.85	57.87
Beneficial Corp., Wilmington, Del.	1,497,535	2.60	60.47
AVCO Financial Services, Inc., Newport, Calif.	1,360,249	2.34	62.81
International Harvester Credit Corp., Chicago, Ill.	1,266,234	2.20	65.01
Montgomery Ward Credit Corp., Wilmington, Del.	1,158,031	2.00	67.01
J.C. Penny Financial Corp., Wilmington, Del.	1,043,334	1.80	68.81
Walter E. Heller International Corp., Chicago, Ill.	1,007,410	1.70	70.51
Westinghouse Credit Corp., Pittsburgh, Pa.	852,235	1.50	72.01
Transamerica Financial Corp., Los Angeles, Calif.	677,918	1.20	73.21
GAC Finance Inc., Allentown, Pa.	613,929	1.10	74.31
James Talcott, Inc., New York, N.Y.	605,500	1.04	75.35
American Investment Co., St. Louis, Mo.	486,329	0.84	76.19
Total Loan Volume for Finance Company Industry	58,100,000	100.00	100.00

Source: *Financial Institutions: Reform and the Public Interest*, Staff Report of the Subcommittee in Domestic Finance, Committee on Banking and Currency, House of Representatives, August 1973.

minority and minority populations. Although it would be foolish to
expect the Hunt Commission to make recommendations which would
wholly alleviate the wealth and income deficiencies between the
minority and non-minority populations, the Commission could have
suggested ways of making the financial system more socio-economically
efficient.[11]

Although finance companies are an important source of credit, they remain
relatively unregulated. Federal charter requirements have been waived on the
basis that state regulatory agencies do an adequate job. However, in actuality,
this is not the case, because state regulations generally lack uniformity and
consistency.

Debtor harassment is another area in which consumers could benefit by
federal and/or state regulation. Sometimes consumers choose to be delinquent in
making their credit payments or to stop the flow of payment completely. They
do so for various reasons, which include shoddy merchandise, warranties that
are informally or formally not honored by the seller, and deception regarding the
price of the merchandise or its expected quality.

Without question, creditors have a legitimate right to expect to be paid.
However, occasionally the tactics creditors use against minority debtors are un-
necessary; they go beyond the bounds of propriety—and occasionally, of legality.
Collectors have been known to make phone calls that were either abusive or so
frequent or at such late hours that they were highly demeaning and without
justifiable sanction. Collectors also frequently contact a debtor's employer,
threaten garnishment of wages, or threaten legal action—all of which constitute
harassment and a psychic cost which is not calculated into the cost of credit. In
most situations, minorities have little recourse in as much as federal and state
regulatory agencies are still several leagues away from offering debtors refuge
from the carry-over of draconian types of harassment.

Alternative Sources of Credit

During the latter 1960s, the Federal Trade Commission (FTC) undertook a
study to help eliminate deception in marketing and credit practices in inner
cities, and to determine if credit abuses were more common among inner city
residents.[12] The study, which examined the District of Columbia, focused on the
following issues: (1) the margin of sales made through installment credit, (2)
price schedules in inner cities markets as compared to those in outer city market
areas, (3) gross margins of inner city retail outlets,[b] (4) the cost of inner city

---

[b]The term "gross margin," in the context of this study, is intended to mean the difference between the wholesale and the retail price, as a percentage of the wholesale price.
This is the amount that remains for covering a retailers' operating expenses, including

borrowing, (5) the relationship between retailers and finance companies, and
(6) legal actions taken by retailers in delinquent installment contracts, and (7)
the socioeconomic characteristics of inner city residents.

Due to the study's emphasis on credit in the inner cities, this discussion will
only deal with some of these issues in detail, while it will deal with others in a
heuristic fashion.

The FTC survey included 96 retailers with combined sales of $226 million
annually. This roughly approximated eighty-five percent of the total sales of
appliance, furniture, and department store retailers in the District of Columbia.
The FTC study focused primarily on installment credit contracts because of the
difficulty in collecting data on revolving credit accounts, which are generally
continuing credit arrangements [c]

The study disclosed that retailers' dependence on credit sales varied considerably from discount appliance stores, which made few sales on credit, to
others which conducted all their sales transactions on a credit basis. Also, the
percentage of "markup" varied widely among retailers. The type of outlet did
not determine the type of practices.

Credit Sales

A salient characteristic of the inner city is the high percentage of sales by
retailers conducted on installment credit. Table 2-9 shows that sales on installment credit amounted to 92.7 percent of the total sales of inner city retailers. In
contrast, the installment credit of "general market retailers," whose operations
were based outside of the ghetto amounted to only 26.5 percent. Thus, the factor that distinguishes inner city merchants is that more than 90 percent of their
sales are transacted on credit, indicating that additional purchasing power is
needed both for the viability of the merchant and for the ability of the inner
city resident to consume.

Prices and markups are typically higher among retailers located in minority
areas. In Tables 2-10 and 2-11, we see that the retail price schedule of inner city
merchants is the highest as a result of higher gross margins.

Installment Credit

The average value of a contract for an inner city merchant was $140, as
can be seen in Table 2-12. The practices involving installment credit, for the

---

salaries, commissions, rental charges, equipment costs, other overhead expenses, and net
profits. Also, within the context of this study, the term "general retailer" will refer to retail
establishments located outside of the inner city.

[c]The exclusion of this type of credit allowed simplification of the investigation, and it
was reported that it did not create any significant biases in the results.

Table 2-9

Value of Installment Contracts as Percent of Sales, District of Columbia Retailers, 1966

			Installment Contracts:		
Type of Retailer	Number of Companies	Net Sales (In Thousands of Dollars)	Value (In Thousands of Dollars)	Percent of Total	As Percent of Net Sales
Total	65	$150,970	$45,251	100.0%	30.0%
Low Income Market Retailers	18	7,874	7,296	16.1	92.7
General Market Retailers	47	143,096	37,955	83.9	26.5
Appliance, Radio, and Television	22	25,089	8,466	18.7	33.7
Furniture and Home Furnishings	22	26,643	10,608	23.5	39.8
Department Stores	3	91,364	18,881	41.7	20.6

Source: *Consumer Credit and the Poor:* Hearing Before the Subcommittee on Financial Institutions of the Committee on Banking and Currency, United States Senate, 90th Congress Second Session on The Federal Trade Commission Report on Credit Practices (Washington: U.S. Government Printing Office, 1968), p. 47.

Table 2-10

Average "Retail Prices" of District of Columbia Retailers on Best Selling Items of Appliances and Furniture in 1968, Assuming Wholesale Cost of $100 for Each Item[a]

	Average "Retail Price" Assuming $100 Wholesale Cost			
	Low Income Market Retailers	General Market Retailers:		
Merchandise Item		Appliance Stores[b]	Furniture Stores[b]	Department Stores
Television Set	$187	$131	$140	$134
Carpet	200	—	160	150
Refrigerator	202	132	133	153
Washing Machine	204	133	148	155
Stereo-Phonograph	211	149	157	153
Freezer	216	133	—	151
Dryer	217	135	138	160
Furniture	228	—	190	202
Vacuum Cleaner	237	136	143	157
Radio	250	130	161	139
Sewing Machine	297	196	—	174

[a]These are cash prices and do not reflect separately imposed finance charges.

[b]Appliance and furniture stores have been classified on the basis of their principal merchandise line. Furniture stores carry appliances as a substantial secondary merchandise line, and for this reason average "retail prices" of appliances sold by furniture stores are included in this table.

Source: *Consumer Credit and the Poor*, op. cit., p. 56.

Table 2-11
Comparison of Reported Wholesale and Retail Prices for Best Selling Products, Low Income Market and General Market Retailers

	Wholesale Cost		Retail Price[a]	
	Low Income Market Retailer	General Market Retailer	Low Income Market Retailer	General Market Retailer
Television Sets:				
Motorola Portable	$109.00	$109.50	$219.95	$129.95
Philco Portable	108.75	106.32	199.95	129.95
Olympic Portable	290.00[b]	85.00	249.95	129.95
Admiral Portable	94.00	91.77	249.95	129.99
Radio: Emerson	16.50	16.74	39.95	25.00
Stereo: Zenith	32.99	32.99	99.95	36.99
Automatic washers:				
Norge	144.95	140.00	299.95	155.00
General Electric	183.50	160.40	339.95	219.95
Dryers:				
Norge	80.00	87.00	249.95	102.45
General Electric	206.90	205.00	369.95	237.76
Admiral	112.00	115.97	299.95	149.95
Vacuum Cleaners:				
Hoover Upright	39.95	39.95	79.95	59.95
Hoover Canister	26.25	24.55	49.95	28.79

[a]Retail prices are cash and do not include separately imposed finance charges.
[b]Reported as approximate wholesale cost.
Source: *Consumer Credit and the Poor*, op. cit., p. 58.

Table 2-12
Average Value of Installment Contracts of 65 District of Columbia Retailers, 1968

Type of Retailers	All Contacts	Assigned Contracts	Unassigned Contracts
All Retailers	$146	$264	$117
Low Income Market Retailers	140	298	124
General Market Retailers	147	261	116
Appliance, Radio, and TV	210	212	141
Furniture and Home Furnishings	359	383	332
Department Stores	100	—	100

Source: *Consumer Credit and the Poor*, op. cit., p. 65.

most part, did not involve either finance companies or commercial banks. Instead, the inner city retailer absorbed the credit commitment himself. In contrast, general retailers arranged credit with one or more finance companies or banks. After a credit screening of a customer, the installment credit contract or promissory note was either assigned or discounted. In most cases, the contract

Table 2–13

Installment Contracts Distributed by Effective Annual Rate of Finance Charge (Assigned and Unassigned)[a]

| | Value of Contracts at Each Effective Annual Rate for: | | | | | |
| | Low Income Market Retailers | | General Market Retailers | | All Retailers Combined | |
Effective Annual Rate of Finance Charge (in percent)	Value of Contracts (In Thousands of Dollars)	Percent of Total	Value of Contracts (In Thousands of Dollars)	Percent of Total	Value of Contracts (In Thousands of Dollars)	Percent of Total
33%	$ 360	7.1%	—	—	$ 360	0.8%
29	283	5.6	99	0.3%	382	0.9
27	1,087	21.6	—	—	1,087	2.5
26	685	13.6	—	—	685	1.6
24	—	—	$ 3,541	9.3	3,541	8.2
23	—	—	4,576	12.1	4,576	10.6
22	871	17.3	1,173	3.1	2,044	4.8
20	—	—	16,872	44.4	16,872	39.2
18	1,550	30.8	173	0.5	1,723	4.0
17	—	—	6,311	16.6	6,311	14.7
16	—	—	77	0.2	77	0.2
15	187	3.7	3,210	8.5	3,397	7.9
14	—	—	460	1.2	460	1.1
13	—	—	115	0.3	115	0.3
11	14	0.3	635	1.7	649	1.5
Rate not Available	—	—	713	1.8	713	1.7
Total	$5,037	100.0%	$37,955	100.0%	$42,992	100.0%

[a]Includes all installment contracts for which separate finance charges were specified.

Source: *Consumer Credit and the Poor*, op. cit., p. 69.

assignment took place at either the time of purchase, the time of delivery, or before the first payment was due.[d]

Finance companies held all of the installment contracts for appliance retailers, whereas commercial banks held the greatest portion of contracts for furniture transactions, which amounted to 64 percent. Even though ghetto merchants

---

[d]When a retailer assigned a contract, the customer's financial obligation was transferred to the "holder in due course" and the borrower's legal obligation to the financial intermediary which held the contract, regardless of any disputes which might arise over the quality of the product or service. For example, in a separate, but in a sense a somewhat related incident during the early 1960s, there was an organized effort made by exercise and health studios to sign up people for lifetime memberships, which would entitle them to use the exercise facilities for the remainder of their lives without incurring any further costs. Shortly after this, many of these health studio chains and independents entered into receivership, which negated future use of the facilities. Nevertheless, people who had chosen to take out life memberships and to finance them through installment credit were held responsible for honoring the full debt commitment.

transacted more than 90 percent of the sales on a credit basis, they only assigned 20 percent of their contracts and held the other 80 percent. Typically, they held the largest contracts which averaged $298.

Finance Charges

Retailers who operated in the ghetto and did not treat finance charges separately in calculating the payment schedule due on an installment contract, typically priced their goods at 3 times the value of other outlets. Their prices were even higher than other inner city merchants who would figure out the cost of credit and tag it on to the sales price. Some retailers would use "add-on" rate charts for determining the monthly payment schedule. No allowance was made for the fact that the credit balance was diminishing over the time period, and as a result, the "add-on" charge did not represent the true effective cost of borrowing. The effective annual rate minority households were paying was double the add-on rate. Table 2–13 discloses most of the credit sales by inner city merchants had effective credit charges of 22 percent or more. Approximately half of the installment purchases made by minority consumers had to be financed at rates which ranged from 26 to 33 percent. In contrast, credit finance charges by general market retailers outside the ghetto seldom exceeded 20 percent. This was generally true for seventy-five percent of the group. Only a fraction of 1 percent of the general market retailers had borrowing charges which exceeded 24 percent. In Figure 2–4, we see the distribution of the credit charges associated with inner city and general retail sales transactions.

Credit Harassment and Repossesion

In examining the problems minorities experience with judgments, garnishments, and repossessions by inner city retailers, the FTC study found that 12 percent of the ghetto merchants obtained 2,690 judgments which resulted in 1,568 garnishments and 306 repossessions. These results can be seen in Table 2–14.

General market retailers who conducted their businesses outside of the inner city had markedly lower numbers of judgments, garnishments, and repossessions. The non-inner-city retailers that were surveyed reported only 70 judgments for the year, a figure which approximated the number of judgments ghetto merchants would obtain within the course of one week. The FTC study cited that one large department store, whose sales had vastly exceeded the total volume for the entire low income market group, reported 29 judgments for the year.

In investigating the practices of general retailers, the FTC found that they generally avoided turning to the courts for credit collection either directly or

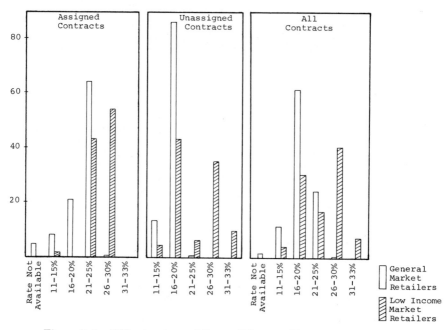

Figure 2–4. Effective Annual Rate of Finance Charges by Inner City Merchants.

Table 2–14
Judgments, Garnishments, and Repossessions on Delinquent Installment Contracts Reported by District of Columbia Retailers, 1966

Type of Retailers	Number of Retailers Reporting	Total Judgments	Judgments Resulting in:	
			Garnishments	Repossessions
Low Income Market Retailers	11	2,690	1,568	306
General Market Retailers:				
Appliance, Radio, and Television Retailers	3	—	—	3
Furniture and Home Furnishings Retailers	8	70	26	13
Department Stores	1	29	9	—
Total	23	2,789	1,603	322

Source: *Consumer Credit and the Poor*, op. cit., p. 75.

Table 2-15

Debt Suits Filed in the District of Columbia by Low Income Market and General Market Retailers, 1966

Type of Retailers	Number of Suits Filed	Number of Retailers	Net Sales 1966 (In Thousands of Dollars)	Net Sales per Debt Suit
Total Sample of Low Income and General Market Retailers	3,646	65	150,970	41,406
Low Income Market Retailers	3,030	18	7,874	2,599
General Market Retailers:	616	47	143,096	232,299
Appliance, Radio, and Television	53	22	25,089	473,377
Furniture and Home Furnishings	207	22	26,643	128,710
Department Stores	356	3	91,364	256,640

Source: *Consumer Credit and the Poor*, op. cit., p. 76.

indirectly much more frequently than inner city merchants (refer to Table 2-14). The conclusion we can draw from the FTC survey is that taxpayers are risk underwriting and subsidizing some of the ghetto merchants, since the courts serve as the credit collection arm of these merchants. This is not only a burden on the courts, but on the tax system as well, not to mention the social costs incurred by the inner city.

3

Capital Markets and Nonbank Financial Intermediaries and the Inner Cities

One of the ways to obtain clearer insight into capital market activities and the role of nonbank financial intermediaries in the inner cities is to examine how the flow of funds process is influenced and directed by government supported funding programs—in particular, the Small Business Administration, and the Minority Enterprise Small Business Investment Companies. These organizations will be discussed, not only to assess their programmatic aims and economic performance, but also to shed light on their underlying philosophies.

The Small Business Administration

Purpose

The Small Business Administration is a permanent, independent government agency created by Congress in 1953 to encourage, assist, and protect the interests of small business.[1] Congress directed the SBA to take the lead role in identifying and analyzing small business problems, to be the voice and advocate of small business, to foster and coordinate research and organization of significant data, and to initiate ideas and innovations that would provide opportunities for small businesses to get started and compete on an equitable basis.

The case usually made in support of special financial assistance programs for small business rests upon the observation that there are imperfections in financial markets. These imperfections result in the allocation of less capital to the largest-in-number but smallest-in-size segment of the economy's business sector. This observation provides the underlying theme of the Small Business Act, which authorized assistance to small firms when financing is not available "on reasonable terms."

In 1958 the Federal Reserve System conducted a comprehensive study to determine the needs and the adequacy of small business financing.[2] Its findings indicated that there is an unfilled gap between the volume of funds available to small businesses in general, especially for new firms, and the volume that could be employed without prohibitive risk.

Two other empirical investigations have been conducted on the issue of financing small business. The research work of one group concluded that banking institutions are capable of meeting the short-term loan demands of small firms,

53

but they are not able to supply, nor do they have the capacity to correct inadequacies in, intermediate- and long-term financing.[3] In contrast, the other study's evidence showed just the contrary. It concluded that small businesses had received too much debt and at a relatively low price compared to the cost of equity.[4]

This diversity of opinion is probably in part caused by the lack of a clear definition of what constitutes "capital gap" and funding deficiency. A capital gap may be said to exist (1) if the marginal return on funds invested in small firms exceeds the marginal cost of capital, or (2) if the cost of funds for small concerns is higher than the cost of funds for other firms in general. Either one or both of these conditions must be satisfied for a capital gap to exist.

A recent study, concerned with the second condition, reached the conclusion that there was no small business equity gap.[5] However, research conducted by the SBA's Planning, Research, and Analysis Department reported just the opposite findings through use of the first criterion.[6] Its findings indicate that there is significant evidence of small business capital gaps with respect to intermediate- and long-term credit. This investigation reviewed the SBA's loan program from its inception in 1953 through December 1967. Using the financial reports of some 22,000 borrowers, it assessed their achievements year by year after receiving a loan. For purposes of measurement, it used principal measures of economic growth, such as profits, sales, assets, and net worth. Its results indicated that borrowers, in the aggregate, experienced a significantly more rapid growth in profits than industry growth averages over the same time period. The other growth indicators—sales, assets, and net worth—also revealed generally superior performances by the borrowers included in the sample. The study also conducted a cost-benefit analysis of the loan program, and results indicate that the equivalent internal rate of return on the loans was approximately 15 percent. This suggests that the borrowers, who, by definition, had been unable to obtain financing elsewhere "on reasonable terms," yielded returns on invested capital which equalled or surpassed the returns that might have been expected from alternative uses.

The results, coupled with other observations of financial problems of small firms, have confirmed the SBA's belief that the capital gap does exist, especially with respect to intermediate- and long-term financing. An added dimension to the problem is that smaller firms rely largely upon the commercial banking system, which is often reluctant to satisfy their financing needs, rather than upon organized national capital markets.

The reluctance of commercial banks to satisfy the capital needs of small concerns is attributable primarily to the liquidity problems associated with intermediate- and long-term debt instruments. Some efforts have been made to cope with this problem by establishing secondary markets for such instruments, but the results have not yet been sufficient to significantly narrow the capital gap.

Capital Deficiencies

If a capital gap is a problem for small firms per se, it is not difficult to understand why an even greater gap might exist for minority firms, which labor under the additional constraint of discrimination. To illustrate the extent of the capital gap for minorities, let us consider the equity position of minorities. In 1969, Black-owned businesses totaled 163,000. This was 2.2 percent of the 7.3 million business firms. The total gross sales of Black companies was $4.5 billion, constituting 1.5 percent of the sales of all industrial corporations.

The White-to-Black population ratio is 8.8 to 1. The White-to-Black business ownership ratio is 46 to 1, and the White-to-Black business dollar ratio is an indigent 336 to 1! The majority of Black-owned businesses are small retail and service outlets.

If proportionate participation of Blacks in business ownership were assumed, then Blacks would own 11.3 percent of 7.3 million businesses, or 820,000. That represents an increase of 657,000 businesses, with gross sales of $170 billion. Further, if an average capitalization of $35,000 were assumed for each of the 163,000 Black-owned businesses in addition to the 657,000 increase, a capital investment of $30 billion would be represented. This analysis serves to illustrate the magnitude of the minimum financing required to begin to alleviate the ownership disparity. Significant gains will not be realized until financing of Black business units occurs at levels of $1 million and above.[7]

In 1969, it was estimated that about 4 percent of the nation's firms were in the inner cities. Even if all were minority-owned, minorities would still be grossly under-represented in the business sector. If any noticeable change is to take place, minority enterprise programs must reach beyond the inner city and into the nation's business mainstream to upgrade both the location and industry distribution of minority-owned enterprises, since in most instances it is automatically expected that minorities should locate in the inner cities and concentrate on solely servicing that area.

Just as the previous studies described pertained to small firms in general, there were additional investigations conducted by the SBA to determine the adequacy of finance as perceived by minority persons, and to determine the geographic variation in performance using a bank participation loan index.[8] This index was constructed so that a district which contained the same percentage of the national minority population as its share of all loans to minority persons was assigned an index of 100. That is, it was considered to be performing at the national norm. Indices exceeding or falling below 100 revealed the degree to which a district exceeded or fell short of the national norm. The results are summarized in Tables 3-1, 3-2, and 3-3.

Table 3-1 indicates that, of all the heads of household interviewed, only 5 percent were in business, 37 percent had not even considered entering business,

Table 3-1

The Capital Gap As Perceived by Minority Heads of Households

	All Heads of House- holds (percent)	Income $15,000 and over (percent)	With 1 to 3 Years College (percent)
Established Business	5%	17%	15%
Had Not Considered Starting a Business	37	39	39
Had Considered Starting a Business	58	44	46
Reasons for Not Entering into Business:			
Finance	72	64	74
Other	28	36	26

Source: Derived from Garvin W.J. "The Small Business Capital Gap: The Special Case of Minority Enterprise," *Journal of Finance*, Vol. 26, No. 2 (May 1971), p. 450.

and 58 percent had considered entering business. However of these 58 percent who had considered entering business but were not in business, 72 percent cited lack of capital as the principal barrier to entry.

A similar response pattern was observed for respondents with incomes of $15,000 and above, and for respondents classified by the number of years of formal education. The former group, which had the highest percentage (17) in business, had 44 percent who were not in business, of which 64 percent cited lack of financing as the principal obstacle to entry. The latter group had 46 percent who had considered entering business but were actually not in business, of which 74 percent cited finance as the principal deterrent. In summary, the entire spectrum of the Black community, from the poor on one end to the rich and educated on the other end, clearly perceived a capital gap and identified it as the principal reason for not going into business.

Loan Density Index

The loan density index is a measure of lending activity in an SBA district. If in an SBA district the number of loans made to minorities as a percent of the total loans made in the nation equals the district's minority population as a percent of the nation's total population, then the district is assigned a loan density index of 100.

In order to understand the concept of the loan density index, consider a nation with four states, A, B, C, and D, with populations of 100, 75, 40, and 25 respectively. Let each state have a minority population of 20, and let the total number of loans disbursed in a given year be 500. Then the distribution of minorities would be seen as shown below, where the figures in parentheses represent the relative minority population within a state, and those in brackets represent the minority population as a percent of the nation's population.

State A
Total Population: 100
Minority Population: 20
                        (20%)
                        [8%]
Total Loans: 200
Loans to Minorities: 40
Loans to Nonminorities: 160

State B
Total Population: 75
Minority Population: 20
                        (26.67%)
                        [8%]
Total Loans: 150
Loans to Minorities: 40
Loans to Nonminorities: 110

State C
Total Population: 50
Minority Population: 20
                        (40%)
                        [8%]
Total Loans: 100
Loans to Minorities: 40
Loans to Nonminorities: 60

State D
Total Population: 25
Minority Population: 20
                        (80%)
                        [8%]
Total Loans: 50
Loans to Minorities: 40
Loans to Nonminorities: 10

By definition, a loan density index equals 100 if a state receives loans in the same proportion as the proportion of its population to the national population (250). If we assume an ideal situation, then state A has 40 percent of the nation's population and receives 200, or 40 percent, of the 500 loans disbursed in the nation. By similar reasoning, states B, C, and D receive 150, 100, and 50 loans respectively, in accordance to their relative populations of 30%, 20% and 10%.

Further, if we assume that minorities receive an equitable share of the loans disbursed, then since each state has an 8 percent minority population compared to the total population of the nation, each receives 8 percent of the total loans in the nation, or 40 loans. Based on these assumptions, each state has a loan density index of 100, despite the different relative minority populations (20% in state A, 26.67% in state B, 40% in state C, and 80% in state D).

In practice, however, these assumptions of ideal conditions are not realized. Although ideally minorities in states C and D, with high relative minority populations, should receive 40 of the 100 loans and 40 of the 50 loans, respectively, current SBA lending policy deviates far from the ideal conditions. In states with high minority densities, minorities receive far less than their share of 40 loans, and consequently have loan density indices far below 100. Good examples of such inequities are San Antonio and Albuquerque, with minority populations of 59.2 percent and 49.9 percent, and loan density indices of only 47 and 52 respectively, as shown in Table 3-2.

Table 3-2
Minority Population Ratio and Loan Density Index by SBA District for 1970

SBA District	Minority Population (percent)	Loan Density Index	SBA District	Minority Population (percent)	Loan Density Index
San Antonio	59.2%	47	San Francisco	18.3%	158
Albuquerque	49.9	52	Dallas	18.0	42
Jackson	41.3	25	Nashville	16.7	43
Marshall	37.6	84	Denver	14.8	446
Columbia	33.4	19	Chicago	14.6	169
New Orleans	31.9	16	St. Louis	14.4	92
Birmingham	29.4	51	Newark	12.4	214
San Diego	29.3	110	Oklahoma City	11.9	55
Phoenix	28.2	97	Philadelphia	11.8	97
Atlanta	27.6	43	Detroit	11.7	205
Houston	27.6	78	Columbus	8.8	98
Washington, D.C.	27.1	33	Cleveland	8.3	147
Charlotte	25.1	50	Hartford	8.3	193
Richmond	23.0	51	Kansas City	8.3	216
New York City	20.9	67	Louisville	7.3	139
Los Angeles	20.9	70	Indianapolis	6.7	242
Little Rock	20.5	23	Seattle	6.4	226
Jacksonville	19.6	53	Pittsburgh	4.2	349
Miami	19.4	114	Syracuse	3.4	551
Baltimore	19.0	45	Boston	3.4	792

Source: Derived from Garvin W.J. "The Small Business Capital Gap: The Special Case of Minority Enterprise," *Journal of Finance*, Vol. 26, No. 2 (May, 1971), p. 452.

On the other hand, in states with relatively small minority populations—states A and B in the illustration given above—the inequity in loan disbursement seems to favor minorities who receive more than a fair share of the 40 loans. However, this is not significant enough to offset the other disproportion. Table 3-2 indicates that Boston and Syracuse are two districts which illustrate this point. In fiscal year 1970, Boston and Syracuse had relative minority populations of only 3.4 percent each. Yet, the loan density indices for these two districts were 792 and 551, the highest two in the nation.

Table 3-2 also ranks relative minority population for SBA districts with the 40 highest loan density indices in the nation. Ranking and correlation between the relative minority population and loan density index, which yields a correlation coefficient of -0.55, indicates that those districts which had the highest minority population as a percent of their total population, had relatively low loan density indices. This means that minorities did not receive an adequate or a proportional amount of total loans. As stated previously, San Antonio had a minority population of 59.2 percent, and a loan density index of only 47. This implies that although it had a large number of minorities, particularly Mexican-Americans, it did not supply them with adequate financing.

Participation growth rates over the 1969–70 period did not show any strong correlation with either loan density index (-0.14) or minority population (+0.18), as can be seen in the following correlation matrix.

	MP	*PG*	*LDI*
Minority Population (*MP*)	1.00	0.18	-0.55
Participation Growth (*PG*)	0.18	1.00	-0.14
Loan Density Index (*LDI*)	-0.55	-0.14	1.00

This implies that over this time period there was no clearly observable relationship between a district's minority population or its loan density index and changes in lending activity. That is, a district with a high minority population density did not necessarily enjoy a substantial increase in loan disbursements, thus indicating that lending policies do not take minority population density into consideration. For example, San Antonio had a minority population of 59.2 percent, and a participation growth rate of 130 percent. On the other hand, the District of Columbia also had a relatively large minority population of 33.4 percent, but experienced a 19 percent decrease in the number of loans, as shown in Table 3-3.[a]

Also, analysis of percentage growth rates in banks participation and loan density indices indicate that there was a very wide range variation from a low of

---

[a]Notable exceptions were Oklahoma City, Los Angeles, and Baltimore, which had either extremely large decreases in the number of loans in spite of relatively large minority populations, or *vice versa*.

Table 3-3

Minority Ratio and Bank Participation Growth Rate by SBA District—Fiscal Year 1969-1970[a]

SBA District	Minority Population (percent)	Participation Growth Rate (percent)	SBA District	Minority Population (percent)	Participation Growth Rate (percent)
San Antonio	59.2%	130%	San Francisco	18.3%	77%
Albuquerque	49.9	36	Dallas	18.0	36
Jackson	41.3	5	Nashville	16.7	40
Marshall	37.6	267	Denver	14.8	68
Columbia	33.4	(19)	Chicago	14.6	92
New Orleans	31.9	140	St. Louis	14.4	14
Birmingham	29.4	14	Newark	12.4	86
San Diego	29.3	108	Oklahoma City	11.9	300
Phoenix	28.2	38	Philadelphia	11.8	(8)
Atlanta	27.6	(14)	Detroit	11.7	79
Houston	27.6	41	Columbus	8.8	(45)
Washington, D.C.	27.1	6	Cleveland	8.3	7
Charlotte	25.1	34	Hartford	8.3	(14)
Richmond	23.0	(6)	Kansas City	8.1	(10)
New York City	20.9	46	Louisville	7.3	64
Los Angeles	20.9	98	Indianapolis	6.7	8
Little Rock	20.5	0	Seattle	6.4	71
Jacksonville	19.6	6	Pittsburgh	4.2	9
Miami	19.4	(8)	Syracuse	3.4	15
Baltimore	19.0	(64)	Boston	3.4	42

[a]Note parenthesis are used to denote negative values.

Source: Derived from Garvin W.J. "The Small Business Capital Gap: The Special Case of Minority Enterprise," *Journal of Finance*, Vol. 26, No. 2 (May, 1971), p. 453.

negative 64 percent in Baltimore to a high of a positive 300 percent in Oklahoma City. As can be seen, some of the twenty lowest-scoring districts, like Marshall, Los Angeles, Oklahoma City, San Antonio and New Orleans, had exceptionally large increases in the number of bank participation loans. On the other hand, New York City, Atlanta, Baltimore, Richmond, and Columbia were also in the low scoring group, despite having low loan density indices.

On the whole, while loan density indices appeared to be inversely related to the minority population of districts, there was not sufficient evidence to sustain the hypothesis that a relationship existed between the relative volume of participation loans and the rate of change of loan volumes. Though studies have not yet been conducted, the inverse relationship may be due to the fact that high loan densities and growth rates are associated with abnormally high risks. In other words, high loan density districts may attract a high proportion of borrowers who are not necessarily successful entrepreneurs and who have little chance of success in business.

The issue of successful entrepreneurs introduces an important element into the discussion of financing minority enterprise. The argument is often made that the main problem is not capital, but lack of sufficiently qualified business ownership candidates. While this may have been true in the past, Figure 3-1 indicates that this argument is no longer valid.

Figure 3-1 depicts minority employment as a percent of total employment for the period 1958-1969. The upper solid line on the chart depicts minority white collar workers as a percentage of the total number of workers. This line, during the 11-year span, indicates that the ratio of minority persons rose from

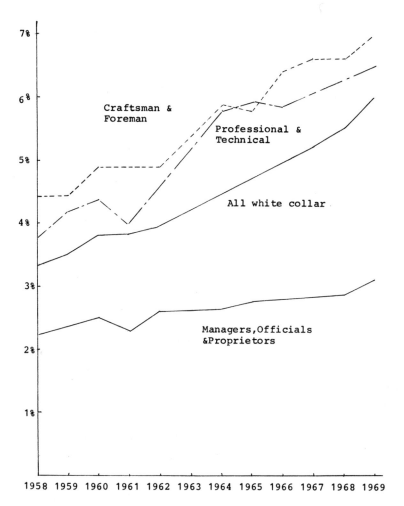

Figure 3-1. Minority Employment as Percentage of Total Employment According to Occupational Categories.

3.2 percent to 6.0 percent. Similarly, the ratio of minority professional and technical workers, indicated by the broken line, has increased from 3.8 percent in 1958 to 6.5 percent in 1968. In contrast with these, minority employment in the manager, officials, and proprietors categories has increased only from 2.3 percent in 1958 to 3.2 percent in 1969. Most of the increase occurred between 1967 and 1969. Assuming continued emphasis on training programs and continued improvement in the education of minorities, this trend should be more pronounced in the future and should close the alleged candidacy gap.

Inner Cities Financing

In 1968, the federal government established a new program, Project OWN, which was to supplement existing programs aimed at fostering the growth and development of the minority-owned business community. Since the SBA was the principal agency of the federal government involved in financing minority enterprise, the government increased the SBA's lending activities and its loan guarantee program. During the six-year period ending June 30, 1973, the SBA approved nearly 40,000 direct loans and bank loan guarantees, providing over $1.1 billion to minority entrepreneurs.[9]

This section examines the trend in SBA financing over the four year period 1970–1973, by ethnic groups, after a brief background of the development of Project OWN and its successor, Operation Business Mainstream.

In January 1964, the SBA established the "6×6" program, an experimental program intended to assist owners of very small service and retail firms who were identified as disadvantaged. The program received the name "6×6" since the SBA set a loan ceiling of $6,000, and offered maturities for up to 6 years. The SBA also established the program with the implicit understanding that minorities would receive a large share of the loans granted.

During the program's first year of operation, 393 of the 794 "6×6" loans approved—approximately half—were granted to minority firms. On this basis, the program was considered to be a success and therefore expanded in 1965 into the Economic Opportunity Loan (EOL) Program, which was authorized under Title IV of the Economic Opportunity Act.[b]

Under this new program, which sought to assist the poverty stricken, loan eligibility criteria were modified to be determined by the borrower's family income in relation to the number of dependents. Also, the $6,000 ceiling was raised to $25,000 and the 6-year limit extended to 15 years.

A year later, in 1966, Title IV of the Act was amended. This resulted in extension of the EOL Program to include people with incomes above the poverty

---

[b]The discussion throughout this section has evolved from a recent study by Timothy Bates, "Trends in Government Promotion of Black Entrepreneurship," *The Review of Black Political Economy,* Vol. 5, No. 2 (Winter 1975), pp. 175–184.

level who had been denied the opportunity to compete on equal terms in business. By July 1968, EOL loans approved increased to 7,628, with a total dollar value of $80 million. Minorities received 40 percent of these loans, both in terms of number and dollar amount.

Also in July 1968, under Director Howard Samuels, the SBA further altered the EOL program. It established Project OWN to create and expand all lines of minority business, not just businesses owned by people living in poverty. The purpose of Project OWN was to narrow minority communities' ownership gap. Thus, the percentage of EOL loans to minorities increased from 40 percent in fiscal 1968, to 67 percent in fiscal 1970, and further to 71.9 percent in fiscal 1971.

In correspondence with the goals of the new Project, the SBA eased lending criteria in all its financial assistance programs, as well as in guaranteeing bank loans to minorities.

In his 1968 presidential campaign, Richard Nixon stressed the importance of promoting Black Capitalism as his Black business development strategy and the emphasis of his civil rights program. This emphasis was actually embodied in the continuation of Project OWN under the new name of Operation Business Mainstream.

Under its new name, the program underwent two significant changes. First, SBA loan approval procedures were simplified and a guarantee arrangement was established which minimized the paper work involved in obtaining SBA guarantees for bank loans. Second, the proportion of equity financing required in borrowing was lowered for minorities, and rules prohibiting loans to finance a change in ownership of a firm were relaxed.

Within the framework of this historical perspective, the following section examines the SBA's financing of minority firms. The discussion will center on work conducted by Bates through his use of SBA direct loan and guaranteed loan data obtained from the SBA regional offices in five major cities—Washington, D.C., Philadelphia, New York, Chicago, and Boston.[10]

In examining changes which took place during the two fiscal years 1968 and 1969 in the five cities under consideration, we see that direct loans and loan guarantees to Blacks and other minority groups increased sharply in fiscal year 1969 from 251 to 635 for Blacks, from 46 to 128 for other minorities, and from 255 to 362 for Whites. Other minorities and Blacks show the most pronounced increases, with Blacks receiving the major share of direct loans and loan guarantees.

In 1970, under Operation Business Mainstream, the SBA established guarantee arrangement which simplified the process of guaranteeing bank loans. Shortly after this, bank participation increased. During the fiscal year 1969-70, the direct loans to Blacks decreased by 30 percent. On the other hand, SBA guaranteed loans to Blacks increased by 79 percent. During this time period, however, direct loans to other minority groups rose from 84 to 124, and guaranteed bank loans also increased from 44 to 81, indicating a leveling off in

Table 3–4
Number of Approved SBA Direct and Guaranteed Loans in Five Major
Cities, by Race of Borrower 1970-1973

Year	Black	Percent-age Share	Other Minori-ties	Percent-age Share	White	Percent-age Share	Total
1970	685	63%	205	19%	201	18%	1,091
1971	697	53	269	21	345	26	1,311
1972	715	47	345	23	463	30	1,523
1973	740	42	357	20	672	38	1,769
Total	2,837	50	1,176	20	1,681	30	5,594
Percent In-crease 1970–3	8.0		73.3		234.3		62.1
Average Per-centage Share 1970–3		51.3		20.8		28.0	

Source: Timothy Bates, "Trends in Government Promotion Black Entrepreneurship,", *The Review of Black Political Economy*, Vol. 5, No. 2 (Winter 1975), p. 180.

loans to Blacks.[11] This probably resulted from the SBA concern for parity between Blacks and other minority groups, since other minorities make up the 51% of the disadvantaged population.

Table 3–4 shows the number of approved SBA direct and guaranteed loans by ethnic group for the five major cities over the time period 1970-1973. From 1970 to 1973, the total number of loans to Blacks increased by 55 from 685 to 740. This net increase was comprised of an increase of 151 in SBA guaranteed loans and a decrease of 96 in SBA direct loans. Banks were responsible for the entire increase in loans to Blacks during this four-year period.

Bates's findings showed that Blacks had suffered cutbacks, while other minority groups including Chicanos, Eskimos, Asian-Americans, American-Indians, Puerto Ricans and Spanish-surnamed, had enjoyed an increase in the number of loans during this period. Bates's evidence indicated that over the 1970-1973 period, Blacks had an 8 percent increase in the total number of approved SBA direct and guaranteed loans. The corresponding figure for other minorities was 73.3 percent, while for Whites it was 234.3 percent, indicating a rapid expansion in the flow of loans to White-owned firms. The trend in Table 3-4 is considered more pronounced because loans to Whites are typically larger than loans to Blacks and other minority groups. While Bates's conclusions show "that loans to Blacks leveled off in 1970-1973 term period while loans to other minority groups increased rapidly and loans to Whites skyrocketed," this is only partially correct. If we consider the proportional share of loans that each recipient group received over the period 1970 to 1973, we see that other minorities experienced only a modest 1 percent increase in their share of SBA direct and guaranteed loans. Surely this cannot be described as a notable improvement for other minorities, nor can it be viewed as a rapid increase in the number of loans the group is receiving *vis à vis* other participants.

If we examine the percentage share of each racial group over the period examined by Bates, we see that Blacks have usually received the major share of direct and guaranteed loans. When compared to other minorities and Whites, their loan proceeds for the total period amounted to 51.3 percent over the four-year period. It was more than double the amount that other minorities received, even though, as was earlier mentioned other minorities constitute the other half of the minority business community. Blacks' percentage share of loans has been leveling off but not to the benefit of other minorities, since their proportional share does not reflect any significant improvement. In 1970, they were receiving 19 percent. By 1972 they had reached a high of 23 percent, and the following year they fell to 20 percent. Other minorities' percentage share of the total number of direct and guaranteed loans amounted to 20 percent, and their average share over the 1970–1973 interval was roughly the same.

Therefore, Bates' findings show that Blacks over this period did begin to start losing ground, while concurrently other minorities did not improve their situation, and White borrowers steadily increased their relative share of SBA loan proceeds. These conclusions can also be drawn by examining Table 3-5, which shows the racial distribution of SBA loans in terms of dollar volume.

Table 3-5
Dollar Volume and Average Size of SBA Approved Loans, by Race of Borrower (in millions of dollars)

Year	Black	Percent- age Share	Other Minori- ties	Percent- age Share	White	Percent- age Share	Total
Total Dollar Volume							
1970	22.1	59%	4.0	10%	11.4	30%	37.5
1971	23.8	49	5.7	11	20.2	40	49.7
1972	31.8	43	10.2	13	31.7	43	73.7
1973	36.6	31	14.9	12	67.6	57	119.1
Total							
Average Per- centage Share							
1970–73		46		12		43	
Average Size (in dollars)							
1970	34,400		19,383		56,532		
1971	44,576		21,169		58,487		
1972	44,567		29,707		68,549		
1973	49,443		41,641		100,585		

Source: Timothy Bates, "Trends in Government Promotion Black Entrepreneurship," op. cit., p. 180.

Finally, we can concur with Bates's projections that

> If present trends in actual SBA loan approvals persist, increases in the
> proportion of minorities (especially Blacks) in the nation's population
> of business owners will be minimal.[12]

If the trend of the early 1970s does continue, we can expect convergence
to take place between the proportional shares of Blacks and other minorities.
However, because of the stationary state of other minorities, it will inevitably be
at this lower threshold.

The SBA has been accused of shifting more emphasis from Blacks to
Spanish-Americans for political reasons. While this may or may not be true, it
tends to overshadow the real underlying problem of the steady increase in loans
to Whites rather than to minorities in general.

Although the Bates's sample was modest both in terms of the breadth of the
cross section and the length of the time series, there is still one salient inference
that remains in tact. Funding priorities have changed and it appears the SBA's
current interest is to promote entrepreneurship for Whites at the expense of
Blacks and other minorities.

Conclusion

When measured by either number of loan approvals or relative emphasis on
lending to Whites and other minorities, it appears that government efforts to
promote minority business development have stagnated. The SBA's actions over
the four-year period 1970–73 do not seem to be consistent with its policy of
decreasing the ownership gap. Also, as the SBA has shifted from granting direct
loans to guaranteeing bank loans, minority borrowers have had to bear the higher
interest payments associated with the bank financing.

A recent report by the General Accounting Office (GAO) has concluded
that the SBA has used the annual increase in the number and dollar amount of
loans rather than the number of successful minority businesses established, as a
measure of the success of Operation Business Mainstream. While the findings of
this report are discussed in greater detail in the section on Mutual Enterprise
Small Business Investment Companies, it is important to note that if such criteria
are used by the SBA, then its chances of making any substantial contributions to
the economic development of minority business are questionable.

To a large extent the success of SBA programs for assisting minority small
business depends on the success of the EOL program. Unfortunately, the basic
EOL philosophy often requires that the recipients be bad risks. This is evidenced
by the fact that in a nine-month period, new firms with EOLs had a default rate

of 70.2 percent.[13] If such a philosophy is pursued in the future, the SBA will only be perpetuating probable failure among low income, disadvantaged entrepreneurs.

On the brighter side, the SBA is implementing a new program in the form of Small Business Lending Companies (SBLCs) to provide greater financial assistance to the small business community under its existing Loan Guaranty Program. These new lenders will be corporations organized for the single purpose of making loans to small businesses which will be guaranteed in major part by the SBA. A key element in the operation of these lenders will be an ability to sell to institutional investors the guaranteed portion of the loans upon disbursement.

It is perhaps premature to predict the effect of this new program, but whatever its structure and content, unless a concentrated effort is made by the SBLCs to assist minorities, no significant changes in patterns of financing minority small businesses will be seen.

The efficiency and expansion of SBA programs is a reflection of the national political environment, because the SBA's posture towards minority entrepreneurs is an extension of the White House's attitude toward minority concerns in general. What is basically needed is a commitment on the part of not only the federal but also the state and local governments to support minority small business development. With that commitment guaranteed, the major task is to reexamine the objectives and policies of the SBA and to redefine its role to be consistent with its reason for existence.

Minority Enterprise Small Business Investment Companies

MESBIC Development

One of the most important programs that the Small Business Administration spearheaded, in collaboration with the Office of Minority Business Enterprise, is the Minority Enterprise Small Business Investment Company (MESBIC) program. The MESBIC program evolved as a part of the U.S. government's response to surveys that indicated a general lack of adequate sources of equity capital for small firms throughout the country.

In 1958, the U.S. Congress passed the Small Business Investment Act, by which the Small Business Administration was empowered to license investment companies to provide "seed money" or embryonic financing to small enterprises. These investment companies came to be known as Small Business Investment Companies (SBICs). MESBICs,[c] a specialized extension of the SBIC concept, are

---

[c]In government publications, MESBICs are frequently referred to as 301 (d) companies.

private investment corporations that specialize in providing long-term venture capital and management assistance to minority businesses. They may be viewed as quasi-public venture capitalists.[d]

There are currently 69 MESBICs operating in the U.S., with a total private capitalization base of $30–33 million. If we include the private minority venture capital fund, the Urban National Corporation, which has a capital stock of $10 million, the total capitalization of MESBICs currently exceeds $40 million; the average capitalization figure then is $571,429 per firm.

Nonminority SBICs and private venture capitalist groups have added to this capital structure by financially underwriting the ideas and ventures developed and organized by minority entrepreneurs. In addition, the SBA's investment division has provided $32 million in leverage funds as its matching contribution to MESBICs. The matching funds were appropriated in the following manner: $14.5 million of preferred stock, and $17.5 million of debentures.[14]

Earlier, in the fall of 1969, the MESBIC program received a considerable amount of publicity when Maurice Stans announced that the goal of the program was to gain commitments for 100 licenses and operating MESBICs within the first year. However, his projected goal did not materialize. This may be attributed partly to inherent bureaucratic defects in the servicing of the program, and also to the mixed philosophy on which the program was based. The concept of minority capitalism had both liberal and conservative ideological overtones. While it included the belief that minority entrepreneurs are essential to solving the socioeconomic problems of the ghetto, it nevertheless did not lead to an organized effort to reduce unemployment and eliminate the infrastructure problems which plague minority inner cities.

For these reasons and others which will be discussed later in this section, the number of MESBICs and their private capitalization have fallen far short of anticipated figures. In the initial years 1970–71 a total of 36 MESBICs received their licenses. 1971 produced the first MESBIC with $1 million private capitalization. 1971 also witnessed the formation of the greatest number of MESBICs with over $1 million of private capitalization for any year to date. Since that time, however, the growth of MESBICs has declined considerably.

In the years 1972–74 there were only 32 licenses issued, of which only 6 were issued in 1974. Though the reasons for this decline cannot be pinpointed exactly, the decline may be indicative of a less aggressive promotional effort by the MESBIC program than in the initial 1970–71 period. Also, after a few years of the program's operation, investors and the financial community in general may have recognized its basic defects.

---

[d]For further discussion on this joint investment relationship between the private and public sectors, see John R. Dominguez, *Venture Capital* (Lexington, Ma.: Lexington Books, D.C. Heath and Company, 1974), pp. 3–8; "Venture Capital and Venture Business," *Papers and Proceedings,* Annual Meeting of the Association of Nucleus in Japan (Tokyo: Muira Printing Co., January 1973); and *Performance and Prospects of the Venture Capital Industry,* monograph (Beverly Hills: Cantor-Fitzgerald Financial Research Fund, 1974).

Capitalization and Leverage

In the initial years of the MESBIC program, many MESBICs had a private capitalization level of about $150,000. Since 1972 MESBICs have tended to increase their capitalization level, at least partly because the SBA made the regulations regarding the minimal capital required for a MESBIC start-up more stringent. While previously the SBA sanctioned licenses for MESBICs with only $150,000, it presently encourages MESBICs to include funds for operation in their private capitalization; this increases the dollar requirement above $150,000.

The SBA also requires that a MESBIC accumulate at least $500,000 in private funds before the SBA will grant a maximum leverage funding of $3 of long-term subordinated government funds for every dollar of private capital raised. In addition, a MESBIC must have a minimum of $500,000 in private capital before it may become involved in the SBA's preferred stock program.

The consequence of all these regulations and incentives has been an increase in the number of MESBICs with capitalization of $300,000 and more, sponsored by both individuals and business corporations. For example, the six MESBICs licensed in 1974 had a range of initial private investment from $280,000 to $1 million. Of these, two were sponsored by business corporations, including Rockwell International, two were group-owned, and two had community-oriented sponsors.

MESBICs currently have private capitalization of $150,000 to $1,350,000. Of the 69 MESBICs, a maximum of 44 percent have obtained over $500,000 in private funds. 14 other MESBICs have total capitalization levels of over $500,000, including SBA and private funds.

Twenty-seven responses to a recent questionnaire prepared by George Glass to gather statistics on the status of individual MESBICs indicates that thirteen of the respondents have increased the amount of their initial private capital by $10,000 to $625,000.[15] In most of these cases, a high correlation was found between increases of initial private capital and the degree of specific planning by MESBIC management for future capital increases. These specific plans included raising additional private capital by the sale of $50,000 to $2 million worth of stock shares to the parent company, common stockholders, or new participants. In general, however, raising private capital beyond the initial effort is either not very important or a difficult accomplishment for many MESBICs.

From the inception of the program to the period ending October 31, 1974, MESBICs have rendered $31.1 million in financial assistance to 1,256 minority small business firms. Of this $31.1 million, $17.5 million or over 50 percent has been in the form of debt, $9.54 million in the form of debt securities, and $4.0 million in the form of equity securities. Though data for the previous years is not available, in the fiscal year ending March 31, 1974 alone, MESBICs financed 385 or 32 percent of the 1,256 minority firms with $11.0 million consisting of $6.2 million in debt, $3.34 million in debt securities, and $1.54 million in equity securities.

White the facts above emphasize the positive impact of the MESBIC program, less apparent operating difficulties encountered by MESBICs can be seen in the profile of the type of financing done by MESBICs during the fiscal year ending March 31, 1973. That year MESBICs financed a total of 285 small business firms. 55 percent of this financing was in the form of loans; the median loan was $8,000 and the median interest was 8.6 percent.[e] Debt securities accounted for 34 percent, with a median disbursement of $27,000, and a median interest rate of 9.2 percent. Both technical and administrative assistance, which is of prime importance to minority small business, further escalated these operating costs. The government generally does not allocate funds to meet these costs. Furthermore, MESBICs receive small operating revenues because they often take an equity position in the minority-owned small businesses. Even when they assume a debt position, the high failure rate of small businesses in general, and minorities in particular, has left the industry short of adequate operating revenues.

According to the SBA and information received from Glass's MESBIC questionnaire, a total of thirty-six MESBICs have received approximately $32 million from the SBA, of which $8 million were allocated in the fiscal year 1974. The $32 million, comprised in part by $14.5 million in preferred stock, also included $17.5 million in debentures.

Statistics completed by Glass indicate that as of April 1974, no MESBIC had taken advantage of its maximum leverage potential with the SBA. On the contrary, approximately one-half of the institutions responding had opted not to acquire any government subsidy.[16] Yet most of the nonparticipating MESBICs are willing to accept a debt position with the SBA.

The annual cost of SBA debt ranges from $5,200 to $42,000. This indicates that smaller companies may have limited their debt structure to avoid additional debt servicing costs, and in doing so may have affected their operations.

According to data obtained from the twenty-seven MESBICs responding to the questionnaire, the majority of MESBICs have invested approximately 45–50 percent of their available capital at a median value of $350,000. An average MESBIC invested $583,000 or approximately 47 percent of its capital. However, some MESBICs invested less than 33 percent of their available funds, while others invested as much as 80 percent of total available capital. The twenty-seven MESBICs made 406 investments for a total of $14 million of their own money and over $70 million of private funds. Of this, $17 million was equity capital, and $53 million was secured from traditional lending institutions. There seems to be no consistent relationship between the size of the MESBIC, the number of investments or average amount of each investment, and the average capitalization of businesses selected for investment.

---

[e]SBICs made loans at a median interest of 11 percent.

On a median scale, the twenty-seven respondents were fairly successful at maximizing their private capital, averaging a ratio of 5:1. However, a large number of MESBICs received little or no equity capital, which was a major cause of the failure of the MESBIC program. One MESBIC, for example, invested $2.3 million, acquired $11 million in bank money, and received nothing in equity capital. Although this is an extreme case, the average MESBICs financing was comprised of $12.3 million in MESBIC and bank financing, and only $500,000 in equity capital. Overall, the entrepreneur's equity participation equalled approximately 24 percent of total MESBIC capitalization.

Overhead expenses for the twenty-seven responding MESBICs ranged from a low of $15,000 to a high of $400,000; the average was $92,000. On a median scale, the overhead expenses of the twenty-seven responding MESBICs constituted approximately 10 percent of total capitalization. No economies of scale were observed with respect to overhead expenses. The organization allocating $400,000 to its overhead budget had approximately the same percentage of overhead to total capital as the organization with an overhead of $15,000— approximately 5 percent.[17]

Fourteen of the twenty-seven MESBICs received subsidies from parent companies, the Ford Foundation, or OMBE in amounts sufficient to cover total overhead expenses in most cases. Also, income from idle or working assets provided returns to the MESBICs which were usually sufficient to cover overhead expenses.

From the very beginning of the program, the $150,000 private capital figure has been popular, probably because the SBA always considered this to be the legal amount for forming an SBIC. However, there are no restrictions on the size of a MESBIC, and in recent years larger MESBICs have been formed. In comparison to most investment companies, even the larger MESBICs are rather small.

The predominantly small scale of operations presents serious disadvantages for a MESBIC. First, although a few small MESBICs have prospered, a minimum capitalization of $1 million seems to be necessary for ensuring any chance of success. This is because investments made by a MESBIC in minority businesses would probably be less profitable for the first few years, increasing the need for a larger MESBIC to cushion the impact of early losses. Also, a broad capital base is necessary to achieve the diversification of investment portfolio that would increase the possibility of success.[18]

Second, a small scale of operations limits the size of loans or investments a MESBIC can make because statutory requirements limit a MESBIC to committing a maximum of 20 percent of its own capital in any one venture. This means that if a MESBIC is capitalized at $150,000, it can at most commit $30,000 to any one minority business venture, an amount probably not adequate to cover the cost of start-up of a new business. Thus, ventures requiring sizeable capitalization, no matter how profitable they may be, cannot be financed by MESBICs. This is probably why many MESBICs have financed smaller firms in the retail and service-type industries, requiring smaller amounts of private capital.

Last, a small MESBIC capitalization is not sufficient to meet any reasonable overhead expenses. Informal SBA guidelines require an SBIC to have at least two full-time, "sophisticated" managers on its staff before granting a license, even for smaller MESBICs. Personnel costs and the rent for an office alone should cost approximately $50,000 per year to meet these requirements. This represents a third of the total capitalization, and it is absurd to believe that any newly established minority business can generate sufficient cash flows to meet such high expenses. The only way to meet such expenses is for the MESBIC itself to have sufficient capital to bear all or part of these expenses, at least in the early years of operation. This can happen only if it is subsidized by a parent corporation.

Organizational Shortcomings

In an effort to understand the shortcomings of the MESBIC program, one should examine the reason why private investment companies are so reluctant to provide loan and/or equity capital to minority enterprise in spite of the backing by the federal government and the promotion efforts of OMBE. OMBE's own goal in promoting MESBICs is definitely a worthy one: "to foster full equality of access to business opportunities and resources among members of Black, Spanish-speaking, Indian and other minorities." Social responsibility and personal benefit should be adequate reasons for established businesses and the government to assist minorities in achieving this goal. Obviously, no minority economic development can occur without substantial capital. The key question, then, is a practical one: Is the MESBIC program a vehicle that can provide access to sufficient capital?

The answer to this question is self-evident, considering the past performance of the MESBICs and the MESBIC program. Though the intent of the program is good, the operation, and more importantly, the assumptions behind this operation are not.[19]

The MESBIC program was designed with the following assumptions:

1. Proper efforts can attract large sums of "excess capital" from the white community.
2. When white financial institutions lend large sums of money to an emerging minority-owned business, the business will be able to repay the loan, with interest, over a period not exceeding 15 or 20 years.

These assumptions ignore the facts that (1) "white money" is being invited to participate in a risky venture, because of the newness of the business and the start-up problems of the inexperienced minority businessmen, and (b) "white money" is being asked to forego the normal incentive for entering such situations—namely, a higher potential return. In other words, both assumptions ignore the essence of risk premium in business. Furthermore, if high returns do happen to accrue, the assumption is that these earnings will be reinvested into the communities, leaving the white community no share of the profits.

Probably the heart of the problem still lies in the risk involved in financing minority businesses. MESBICs have witnessed not only their own clients' collapse, but also the failure of other federally financed minority businesses. This has deterred them from providing the equity capital that is so essential for minority businessmen. In spite of government efforts to reduce some of the risk by means of guarantees, the high risk/low return investments have obstructed the flow of private capital. Until a workable incentive is found, minority business is certain to be short of badly needed equity capital.

The gap between apparent and actual leverage is another crucial problem with the MESBIC program. The SBA uses leverage to attract private investment companies to participate in minority economic programs. However, the apparent leverage emphasized by the SBA and the actual leverage are not the same. To determine the real leverage provided to MESBICs, let's examine a hypothetical case.

Consider a MESBIC investing $150,000 in a minority business. The total amount generated according to the leverage formula would be $2,250,000. Of this, the additional leverage (hypothesized by OMBE) is $2,100,000. Since the SBA backs the sponsor's investment on a 2:1 basis, $1.00 out of every $7.00 of the additional leverage comes from the SBA. But the other $6.00 must come from loans from private financial institutions to the MESBIC's clients. The SBA is prepared to guarantee 90 percent of the amount of these loans, up to a maximum of $350,000 per venture for any sound loan to a minority-owned small business. The SBA permits such loans to be made on a 4:1 matching basis with equity or other subordinated long-term debt.[20] On this basis OMBE calculates its leverage factor and states that up to $180,000 in loans can be raised on a MESBIC's capitalization base of $450,000.

The flaw in this calculation is that there is no guarantee that banks and other lenders will accept the risks of financing organizations with high debt/equity ratios, even when most of the loan has been indemnified by the government. The experience of Arcata Investment Company testifies to this fact. This corporation, which was a prototype MESBIC, provided $418,500 in loans, guarantees, and direct equity investment for its first 33 clients. Other equity participants matched this combination with $234,000 in equity investments, and the banks put in $814,000. Thus the banks contributed less than $2.00 for every $1.00 contributed by Arcata Investment Corporation. This is nowhere near the highly publicized 15:1 leverage figure.

Actual leverage and the small scale of operations are weaknesses which undermine the viability of a MESBIC as an efficient vehicle of Black capitalism, and hinder its ability to foster minority enterprise on a meaningful scale. Many of the objections to the present program are technically repairable, but in order to have any immediate changes, some legislative actions are necessary to authorize the SBA to guarantee loans directly to a MESBIC, increase the minimum capitalization levels, and decrease the limit on single-venture investments to 10 percent of total MESBIC long-term capital, including bank loans.

With regard to loans, in 1972 an amendment of the Small Business Investment Act of 1958 authorized the MESBICs to issue debentures and preferred stock with the aim of increasing capital available. Nevertheless, there is an acute need for further changes in these statutes.

A key purpose of the needed legislative changes should be to weed out the more "dangerous" business prospects and to increase the probability of locating healthy ventures. Since it is difficult to ascertain exactly what makes a good entrepreneur—for example, why members of a certain Ibu tribe in Africa make successful businessmen, it is worthwhile to examine on a macro-level some of the reasons why federally funded minority businesses have failed.

Success and Failure Rates

In 1973, the General Accounting Office (GAO) issued a report entitled, *Limited Success of Federally Financed Minority Businesses in Three Cities.*[f] Since the federal agencies assisting these businesses, the SBA, OMBE, and the Department of Commerce, had not examined the factors contributing to the success or failure of minority businesses assisted by their programs, the GAO's intention was to determine the success/failure rate and discover underlying reasons.

All of the 845 businesses examined received SBA loans disbursed by the Chicago, Los Angeles, and Washington district offices during fiscal years 1969 and 1970. Of these firms, the GAO classified about 31 percent as "probable successes," 27 percent as "failures," 25 percent as "probable failures," and roughly 17 percent as "undeterminables." These results, which are shown in Table 3-6 were based on the GAO's analysis of a subset of 443 businesses selected randomly from the universe of 845.[21] For purposes of analysis, the businesses were classified by loan repayment status and business operating results. The GAO was unable to locate published statistics on failure rates in all minority and small businesses in the country for comparison.

---

[f]The data represented in Tables 3-6 through 3-10 come from the Report to the Congress, *Limited Success of Federally Financed Minority Businesses in Three Cities,* BL 49685, by the Comptroller General of the United States, November 1973.

Table 3-6
Success-Failure Rates of Minority Firms, Fiscal Year 1969-70

Business Status	Number of Businesses		
	Sample	Projection	Projected Outcome (percent)
Probable Success	137	260	30.7%
Failure	116	232	27.5
Probable Failure	111	213	25.2
Undeterminable	79	140	16.6
Total	443	845	100.0
Probable Failure/Success Ratio (percent)	81.0%	81.9%	82.1%

Source: *Limited Success of Federally Financed Minority Businesses in Three Cities*, op. cit., p. 21.

The 443 minority-owned firms analyzed had received loans of approximately $18.4 million. Of these, 171 had received direct loans, 264 had SBA-guaranteed bank loans, and 8 had both direct and SBA-guaranteed loans. The classifications mentioned above, probable success, failure, probable failure, and undeterminable, were made according to the following criteria.[22]

Probable Success
1. Current in making loan payments and operating at a profit, as indicated by the most recent financial statements which reflect operations for periods after July 1, 1970.
2. Current in making loan payments and having a good payment record. No indications of problems, and a positive statement from either SBA or local bank officers.

Failure
1. Liquidated or in liquidation, and not currently operating.
2. In liquidation and operating at a deficit, with no evidence of being able to reverse the trends, as indicated by either the most recent bank correspondence or the financial statements covering operations.
3. Sold or otherwise disposed of by original borrower because of failure to operate business successfully, despite ability to make regular loan payments.

Probable Failure
1. Delinquent in loan payments (over 60 days past due).
2. Current in making loan payments and operating with a deficit, with no evidence of being able to reverse the trend, as indicated by either the most recent bank correspondence or the financial statements which covered operations for some period after July 1, 1970.

3.   In liquidation and operating without evidence of a recent payment history.

Undeterminable

1.   Current in making loan payments, but no current financial statements available (reflecting operations for some period after July 1, 1970) for SBA inspection. No other evidence of successful operations available.
2.   Deferring current loan payments.
3.   In liquidation and operating with evidence of a recent payment history or a profit, indicated by either the most recent bank statements or financial statements covering operations for some period after July 1, 1970.
4.   Any other set of facts not falling within the above criteria and which cannot be fully analyzed.

The GAO reviewed SBA and bank records and correspondence in order to find evaluations which might indicate reasons for the failure or "probable failure" of aided minority-owned businesses. The results of this investigation are shown in Table 3-7. The GAO also analyzed 443 firms in order to identify relationships which might exist between certain owners, types of businesses, financing methods, and the success or failure of the respective businesses. The GAO found that:

1.   Borrowers using loan funds to purchase existing businesses were more suc-

Table 3-7
Variables Influencing Failure of Minority Firms[a]

Variables	Number of Firms
Inadequate Managerial Capability: heavy operating expenses, difficulties with inventories or receivables, and inadequate sales	155
Operational Neglect: simple negligence, bad health, personal problems, etc.	53
Random Disturbances: acts of God, theft, labor strife, etc.	37
Fraudulent Practices: irregular disposal of assets and false financial statements	25
Extraneous Factors: reasons not covered above, e.g., downturn of the general economy, etc.	54
Unknown	24

[a]This distribution should be viewed with caution since some of the firms in the sample identified more than one cause for failure.

Source: *Limited Success of Federally Financed Minority Businessess in Three Cities*, op. cit., p. 22.

cessful than borrowers using funds to expand their existing businesses or to start new ones.

2. Unfavorable business locations usually resulted in failure.
3. Businesses with bank loans were more successful than businesses with direct SBA loans.

Other characteristics relating to success or failure, though less significant, were the owners' past experience and the equity held in the business.

The GAO analysis indicated that management assistance was provided to only about one-half of the businesses included in its sample that needed assistance. Furthermore, the assistance provided was not beneficial. The analysis also revealed that of the businesses receiving additional loans, 18 percent were classified as probable successes, whereas 56 percent were classified as failures. This indicates that additional loans to businesses did not necessarily enhance the survival rate.

The three factors related to the success or failure rate of minority businesses are discussed below in further detail. First of all, borrowers purchasing existing businesses were more successful. They accounted for 48 percent of the group, as compared to the 25 percent who were starting new businesses or the 26 percent who were expanding businesses. This is shown in Table 3–8. Two possible reasons for this are that (a) a business must have shown profitability before the SBA will make a loan for its purchase; in other words, a viable market for that firm's products must already have been established, and (b) the potential business purchaser has often had managerial experience in the same business he intends to buy, or in a similar business.

Secondly, businesses with unfavorable locations usually fail. The SBA analysis of such factors as market potential, competition in the area, visibility of the business, and extent of crime in the business setting yielded certain conclusions. On the basis of this analysis, the GAO classified the locations for 392 of the 443 businesses as either favorable, unfavorable, or unimportant. As seen in

Table 3–8
Minority Success-Failure Distribution by Type of Venture
(in percent)

Type of Venture and Number of Firms	Probable Success	Probable Failure	Failure	Undeterminable
New Business (113)	25%	22%	27%	26%
Expansion of Existing Business (228)	26	30	29	15
Purchase of Existing Business (102)	48	18	18	16

Source: *Limited Success of Federally Financed Minority Businesses in Three Cities*, op. cit., p. 31.

Table 3-9

Minority Success-Failure Distribution Corresponding to Locational Factors

	Location Classification							
	Favorable		Unfavorable		Unimportant		Inadequate Information	
	Number	Percent	Number	Percent	Number	Percent	Number	Percent
Probable Success	83	33%	8	14%	30	35%	16	31%
Probable Failure	61	25	20	34	22	26	13	25
Failure	61	25	18	30	21	25	11	22
Undeter-minable	43	17	13	22	12	14	11	22
Total	248	100	59	100	85	100	51	100

Source: *Limited Success of Federally Financed Minority Businesses in Three Cities*, op. cit., p. 32.

Table 3-9, 33 percent of favorably located businesses were classified as probable successes. Since most of the minority-owned businesses are in low income, high crime areas, these locations may be only relatively favorable. In contrast, 64 percent of businesses located in unfavorable locations were classified as failures or probable failures, and only 14 percent were classified as probable successes. Therefore, there was a downwards bias in location, in that although favorable location did not guarantee business success, unfavorable location measurably increased the probability of failure.

Thirdly, businesses with bank loans were more successful than those with SBA loans. The percentage of businesses with SBA-guaranteed bank loans which were classified as probable successes was 41 percent. This performance was much better than that of businesses with direct SBA loans, whose percentage of probable success was 16 percent. This is shown in Table 3-10. The percentage of probable failures and indeterminables was similar for both types of loans.

The factors listed above should not be treated in isolation in an attempt to determine reasons for the failure of these minority businesses. They must be considered together with the structural defects of the various SBA and OMBE programs. However, these factors alone have significant implications for MESBICs in establishing policy guidelines and seeking businesses for operation.

The Arcata Investment Company

The Nixon Administration's first major program to aid Black capitalism was launched on November 6, 1969, under the name of Project Enterprise. The heart of this program was commitment of 18 corporations in different parts of the

Table 3-10.
Success-Failure by Type of Loan Financing[a]

Type of Loan and Number of Firms	Probable Success	Probable Failure	Failure	Undeter- minable
SBA Direct Loans (171)	16%	29%	36%	19%
Bank Loans with SBA Guarantee (264)	41	23	19	17

[a]Note that eight of the firms having both bank and direct loans were not included in this sample.

Source: *Limited Success of Federally Financed Minority Businesses in Three Cities*, op. cit., p. 28.

country to form MESBICs that could finance minority enterprises. The proto-type was the Arcata Investment Company, an SBIC formed by Arcata National Corporation of Menlo Park, California in mid-1968. Its purpose was to provide financing and managerial assistance to businesses owned and operated by resi-dents of nearby East Palo Alto, which had an 80 percent representation of Blacks in its population of about 26,000.[23]

In setting guidelines for its operation, Arcata National examined the follow-ing aspects of Arcata Investment Company (AIC):

1. Administrative cost—the overhead accounted for by AIC's salaries, benefits, office space, travel expenses, etc.
2. Bad debt expenses.
3. Cost of capital—the SBA and the parent company charged AIC for the funds made available to the latter for loans and investments.

Arcata Investment Company was expected to cover its cost of capital and any bad debt expenses from interest income, while the parent organization absorbed administrative costs.

One of the most crucial aspects of AIC's program was determining which entrepreneurs to assist. Following an applicant's initial inquiry, Arcata gave him material describing the procedure he should follow to obtain a loan from the Company, and what he could and could not expect. The details of this process, which determined both the applicant's eligibility and the form of the final financing arrangement, are illustrated in Figure 3-2 and summarized below.

First, during the applicant's initial interview, he filled out a personal infor-mation sheet, received a personal financial resume sheet which was to be returned within one week, made arrangements for research, consultants, and anything else that needed to be done to complete his proposal, and established tentative time constraints for the project.

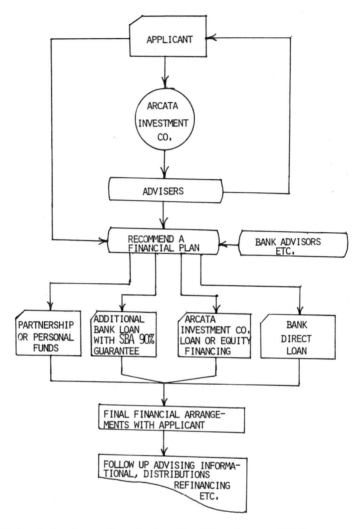

Figure 3–2.   Arcata Consultation Algorithm. Source: J.K. Brown,
"Arcata Investment Company: The Prototype MESBIC," *Conference
Board Record* (April 1970), p. 59.

Second, the applicant developed the following information: (If necessary,
he met with a volunteer business consultant.)

1.   A monthly income and expense statement for one year, and if cash flow was
     significantly different from this statement, a cash flow statement for the
     same time period.

2. Projected income and expense figures for four more years on an annual basis.
3. Records of the sources and uses of funds for starting the business. Also, a list of requirements for opening the business, including additional operating capital if losses were expected for any period of time.
4. Background material that included: (a) assumptions used to derive the figures in projections; (b) possible variations in projections based on changes in volume or assumptions; (c) past experience of owner and employees; (d) market studies made of available customers; (e) marketing and merchandising program; (f) plan for bookkeeper and accounting procedures; and (g) any other information that might be helpful in evaluation, such as names of special advisors or of similar businesses in operation.

Third, the applicant met with Arcata officials to review his proposal. They established a loan program, and, if bank financing was necessary or possible, Arcata contacted the bank to discuss how the financing would be divided between them. Arcata arranged for the applicant to meet with the bank, and set a date by which he should know if the project was approved. If the loan was contingent on bank financing, funds would not be disbursed until bank approval of the request.

Fourth, the applicant met with Arcata to sign loan documents and receive funds. And finally, he made quarterly reports to Arcata, which included a basic income and expense statement. This allowed Arcata to conform to SBA requirements and to offer assistance as the business progressed.[24]

Arcata had several guidelines for evaluating applications. It preferred labor intensive businesses to those with low labor content, and attempted to avoid subsidy of cutthroat competition. It favored an enterprise that would provide a product or a service needed by the community.

Volunteers, who were an important aspect of Arcata's program, helped provide the background information Arcata needed to evaluate applications. They also provided managerial and legal aid to the businesses that received Arcata funds. There were five basic types of volunteers: (a) Vista volunteers, (b) Stanford Graduate School of Business students, (c) Stanford Business School alumnae, (d) business and professional men in Palo Alto, and (e) employees of Arcata National Corporation.

To help prepare the volunteers for their crucial role, Arcata distributed the following guidelines among volunteers:

1. Identify the applicant's personal strengths and weaknesses to aid in evaluation and future plans.
2. Provide Arcata with economic statistics necessary for an intelligent loan decision (including pro forma income and expense statements, capital costs, funds available from the applicant or other sources, risk considerations, growth possibilities, and special expenses or receipts.

3. Identify factors that suggest either a favorable or unfavorable decision regarding the loan. However, Arcata Investment Company takes full responsibility for the loan decision.
4. Provide a communications link between the applicant and bankers, lawyers, insurance companies, specialists in certain fields, and other people whose help the applicant may need.
5. Help provide any information the applicant needs once the business has been financed.
6. Suggest improvements for Arcata's operations.
7. Do not make decisions for the entrepreneur—only offer advice. You need not require or enforce any restrictions or procedures.

Finally, Arcata emphasized that the volunteer's basic role was to prevent minority entrepreneurs from making costly errors or from becoming frustrated as they tried to launch their businesses. The way the volunteer could be most helpful was by getting involved and continuing to show interest in the applicant and his business. "Experts" would be available to help the volunteer in areas where he felt his knowledge was limited, but only he could provide the sustained interest and assistance that was crucial to the minority entrepreneur.

Arcata found that although volunteers were easy to locate, their performance was inconsistent. They were more successful in developing proposals for financing, pro forma income and expense statements, accounting systems and control, than in their follow-up.

Arcata's philosophy about assisting development always involved an emphasis on the responsibility of the entrepreneur, Thus, Arcata did not take a controlling interest in any business, but allowed management and ownership to remain wholly or substantially in the hands of the minorities. Arcata told the entrepreneur that he had a responsibility to himself, to Arcata, and to the community. As long as they could treat the investment as a normal business transaction, they would continue; if they had to think of it as a charity project, they would stop, because then both Arcata and the entrepreneur would have failed—but they anticipated success.[25]

One of Arcata's initial goals was to establish a broadly representative group in East Palo Alto through which it could maintain permanent liaison with the community. Failing to do this, Arcata set up a community screening board to review the initial applications for loans and to send the company only those that met the board's approval. This board, consisting of the head of the local chapter of CORE, an attorney, a minister, and a representative of the local state employment service, appraised a few businesses, but then disbanded because members of the minority community felt that the procedure was unfair. Although the liaison board was disbanded, Arcata did maintain community involvement in its operations.

Ultimately, Arcata became a nonprofitable venture for the same reasons that the MESBIC program was not successful. However, Arcata officers made several observations from their experience which may be useful to the managers of MESBICs now being formed.[26]

1. Arcata should have acted more slowly and with greater caution. It over-reacted to an admittedly great need without careful consideration of businesses.
2. Arcata underestimated capital requirements and the complications of starting a new business in several instances.
3. A syndicate or consortium of investors would have been preferable to a single sponsor. This would not only have spread the risk, but would also have involved broader participation and would therefore have had greater economic and educational impact.
4. A good advertising program was needed for assisted entrepreneurs in order to promote their products and services. This required the establishment of local communication media which are usually absent in minority communities.
5. A formal business education program for assisted entrepreneurs should have been available from the onset to complement volunteer aid.

Realizing its mistakes, Arcata management contended that to achieve the goals of Project Enterprise, the mixture of government and business participation in small business development is superior to both the development of cooperatives and to providing tax incentives. According to Robert Dehlendorf II, the founder, president, and chief executive officer of Arcata Investment Company, banks act as a supplemental source of evaluations and suggestions for improvement of the business and financial package. Also, through constant contact with various minority clients, they develop the ability to identify good minority risks. Bank participation also provides the opportunity for minority businessmen to establish banking relationships which must eventually replace the special sources of financing. In addition, the minority businessmen become accustomed to standard business financial practices rather than to the preferential treatment they receive from MESBICs and the SBA. Even more important, the development of banking ties helps the minority community to establish other banking relationships for nonbusiness needs.

MESBICs and Black Capitalism

In a seminal study Brimmer and Terrell found evidence indicating the ghetto economy does not provide profitable opportunities for small minority firms, that self-employment is risky for Blacks who lack technical and managerial competence, and that a strategy to increase the financial capital available to the

Black business community diverts resources to inefficient enterprises. They further suggested that such Black capitalism strategies discourage Black economic progress by encouraging less than full participation in the American economy. And in an economy in which most persons of comparable status earn salaries and wages, programs of compensatory finance for small-scale entrepreneurial activity have limited economic potential for the Black business community.[27]

Following closely on the heels of the Brimmer-Terrell study was an investigation by Bates in 1973. His empirical survey showed that their results were deficient in several respects. Basing his analysis on financial data gathered from the SBA on new and existing Black firms, Bates concluded that current increases in the supply of financial capital available to the Black business community have been and still are socially productive. Further, due to historically limited access to capital markets, such subsidies are currently necessary if viable Black enterprises are to begin, grow, and prosper.[28]

Shortly after this, Osborne and Granfield, in an effort to synthesize the divergent results of the two previous studies, presented an analytical framework which examined the supply and demand for financial capital in two separate communities, one developed and White, and one underdeveloped and Black. Also, in an effort to determine which, if any, of the hypotheses were valid, they analyzed the performance of 45 Black firms in the investment portfolio of a California MESBIC. Since the subject matter of their entire study is not within the scope of this section, only the results of their analysis and their interpretation will be discussed.[29]

Table 3–11 shows the proportion of Black firms representing certain industrial classifications. Table 3–12 gives a break-down of sales, profits, and total capitalization for various firms in similar groupings. Twenty-five firms were classified as "failed" or "marginal," and 20 firms were identified as solvent and in good condition. Table 3–11 shows that 13 of the total 45 SIC classified Black firms were in transportation, mining, construction, manufacturing, and wholesaling, which can be considered "emerging" lines of Black business activity, as Bates would define them. Thirty-two firms were in retail trade and services, which are the traditional avenues of Black business, as Brimmer would cite.

An examination of successes among the 45 firms in Table 3–11 shows that 46 percent of the 13 firms in emerging lines of business were successes, compared to 44 percent of the 32 firms in the retail trade and service category. Under the "good" classification, 30 percent of the firms in emerging lines were classified as successful, compared to 70 percent in the more traditional retail and service category.

An examination of failures in Table 3–11 shows that 7, or 54 percent of the 13 firms in the emerging industries were classified as failed or marginal. The related figure for the 32 firms in traditional lines was 56 percent. Also, 28 percent of the 56 firms classified as failed or marginal were in the emerging industries, while 72 percent were in the retail industries.

Table 3-11
Status and Industrial Classification of Black Firms in a
MESBIC Portfolio

Standard Industrial Classification and Number of Firms[a]		Operational Status Proportional Frequency	
		Failed and Marginal	Good
Group A:			
Transportation		54%[b]	46%
Mining Construction Manufacturing Wholesaling		28%[c]	30%
Number of Firms	13 (29%)	7 (16%)	6 (13%)
Group B:			
Retail Trade and Services		56%	44%
		72%	70%
Number of Firms	32 (71%)	18 (40%)	14 (31%)
Total Sample Size	45 (100%)	25 (56%)	20 (44%)

[a]Figures in parentheses indicate number of firms as percentage of total portfolio.
[b]Percentages within each group.
[c]Percentages within each status category.
Source: Table was adopted from Osborne, Alfred, Jr., and Michael Granfield, "The Potential of Black Capitalism in Perspective," Unpublished paper, Graduate School of Management, University of California, Los Angeles, 1974, p. 19.

For the entire portfolio, 29 percent of the 45 firms were in the emerging industries, and 71 percent were in the traditional retail trade and service category. Also, 56 percent of the 45 firms were in the failed or marginal category, while 44 percent were classified as successful.[30]

It was stated earlier that of the 32 firms in traditional industries, 56 percent failed. Of these 18 failures, 7 were in the services, and 11 in the retail trades. The higher failure rate in the retail trade industry was consistent with national failure averages for all firms after less than two years of existence. However, the figures were in sharp contrast to Dun and Bradstreet's average failure rates, which revealed that only 25 percent of all failures in retail trades and only 14 percent of all failures in services occur in the first two years. In the 45-firm sample, 56 percent of all retail trade organizations either failed or were failing, while the incidence of failure in the service category was 44 percent. These percentages were far above the national average figure, which supports the Brimmer and Terrell theory.

Table 3-12
Sales, Profit, and Capitalization of Black Firms in a
MESBIC Portfolio by Operational Status and Standard
Industrial Classification

Standard Industrial Classification	Operational Status (and Number of Firms)		
	Failed and Marginal (25)	Good (20)	All Firms
Group A:			
Transportation	$104,310[a]	$170,677	$134,941
Mining	(114,229)[b]	(217,826)	(165,771)
Construction	$ 26,447[c]	$ 33,983	$ 29,925
Manufacturing	(23,893)[d]	(56,627)	(40,458)
Wholesaling	$ 79,042[e]	$170,800	$121,300
(N = 13)	(69,685)[f]	(204,953)	(148,954)
Group B:			
Retail Trade and	$ 95,816	$176,947	$131,311
Services	(116,035)	(197,378)	(159,351)
(N = 32)	$ 15,258	$ 22,688	$ 18,508
	(17,757)	(25,991)	(21,684)
	$ 40,004	$ 69,805	$ 40,385
	(35,706)	(30,520)	(33,016)
All Firms	$ 98,195	$175,066	$132,360
	(113,200)	(197,865)	(159,331)
	$ 18,391	$ 26,077	$ 21,807
	(19,808)	(36,529)	(28,374)
	$ 51,533	$ 79,042	$ 63,759
	(49,230)	(124,391)	(90,525)

[a]Mean Gross Sales.
[b]Standard deviation of Mean Gross Sales.
[c]Mean Profits before taxes.
[d]Standard deviation of Mean Profits before taxes.
[e]Mean Total Capitalization.
[f]Standard deviation of Mean Total Capitalization.

Source: Table was adopted from Osborne, Alfred, Jr., and Michael Granfield, "The Potential of Black Capitalism in Perspective," Unpublished paper, Graduate School of Management, University of California, Los Angeles, 1974, p. 20.

Nevertheless, there is some evidence of successful entry of Black firms into what Bates defined as the emerging lines of business. The national average for failure of 19 percent was far below the 54 percent failure rate in the MESBIC portfolio. However, only 15 percent of the MESBIC firms had definitely failed, which partially supports Bates' hypothesis that Blacks enter emerging business lines with marginal success.

Table 3-12 stresses the important role played by financial capital in the success of firms in emerging industries. Mean total capitalization for firms in this category was $121,300 or three times the corresponding figure of $40,385 for firms in the traditional retail trade and services industry. Firms rated "good" in the emerging industries had mean total capitalization of $170,800, which was approximately $50,000 more than the average figure of $121,300, and over $100,000 more than the average for the entire portfolio ($63,759).

The importance of capitalization as a success factor in transportation, mining, construction, manufacturing, and wholesaling was demonstrated by the fact that the mean total capitalization of $170,800 was over $90,000 more than the average of those firms in the "failed" category ($79,042). Mean gross sales for successful retail and service businesses were found to be twice the sales figure reported by businesses that failed, which supports the Brimmer and Terrell hypothesis that subsidized capital encouraged excess entry, and predictably, they failed. On the other hand, the counter hypothesis was supported by the facts that reported mean profit figures were largest for successful firms in the emerging industries, and average return on sales was greater for firms in the emerging lines, as opposed to the more traditional lines.

As an index of the productivity of invested capital in Black enterprises, Osborne and Granfield examined the ratio of gross profits to total capitalization. Their findings indicated that the average firm earned $21,807 ± $28,374, with sales of $132,360 ± $159,331. This return on sales of 16 percent compared to a mean return of 34 percent on total capital of $63,759 ± $90,525. However, the largest returns on sales within the successful firm category were in the emerging industries (20 percent versus 13 percent), whereas the traditionally protected businesses demonstrated the largest return on capital (57 percent versus 20 percent).[31]

Although this evidence did not support any one particular view, it did show that capital is very important to the successful firms in the emerging industries, while sales and operational efficiency are important to the successful firms in the retail trade and service industries. Capital intensive firms, however, need a longer time horizon to achieve adequate levels of operations before any definitive judgments may be made.

As a final test of the Brimmer and Terrell hypothesis, Osborne and Granfield conducted tests of elasticity of invested funds. They showed that on the average the MESBIC or subsidized capital returns were 4 cents on the dollar.[32] Firms rated successful returned 40 cents beyond the original dollar, which supports Bates's argument. Yet, firms rated as failures and marginals lost 21 cents on the dollar, which supports the Brimmer and Terrell hypothesis. On the average, firms in the retail trade and service industries returned $1.01 on the dollar, while firms in the emerging lines returned $1.17.

These figures indicated that relaxing capital constraints of the Black business community allowed more minority entrepreneurs to enter new lines of business with earnings rates beyond the opportunity cost of capital. They also suggest that such relaxation of constraints simultaneously encouraged excess entry into the already overcrowded retail trade and service industries. Additionally, subsidy capital was found to be a larger proportion (49 percent versus 42 percent) of the capital structure of the failing enterprises than it was of the capital structure of firms in good condition, because most failures occurred in the retail trade and services sector, which is not a profitable area.

Prospects

The vast difference between Maurice Stan's expectations, which were discussed earlier, and the existing number of MESBICs points clearly to the inadequacy of the present program. The emphasis has been placed on numbers— how many $150,000 minimum-sized MESBICs are established and how many small loans they have made. Now, more emphasis is needed on how many MESBICs are adequately capitalized to provide quality service and assistance to disadvantaged businessmen.

In order for any reasonable success to occur, MESBICs must strive for larger capitalization, which will help them to become self-sustaining, viable financial institutions with clients who have the potential of becoming profitable, multi-million dollar companies. There should be sufficient private capital to provide MESBICs with adequate income from idle funds to cover operating cost, while at the same time allowing them to make timely investments in small businesses without depending on immediate interest or principal repayment. To be sure, the industry will not achieve any healthy growth rate if it relies only on making high risk loans and growing from interest income. Therefore, equity type investments with capital appreciation are vital for long-term survival.

Also, changes in existing statutes and regulations are definitely needed. The Small Business Investment Act of 1958 was amended in 1972 so that MESBICs were authorized to sell preferred stock and/or debentures to the SBA. Section 303 (c) (1) of the Act, which was added as a result of the 1972 amendments, authorized the SBA to purchase nonvoting securities of certain 301 (d) licenses. The dividends on these securities are preferred and cumulative to the extent of 3 percent of par value per annum. Under the present statute, the SBA is authorized to require the preferred payment of the difference between dividends computed at a rate determined pursuant to Section 303 (b) and the 3 percent dividend prior to any distribution of the licenses.

Section 303 (c) (2) of the Act authorized the SBA to purchase and/or guarantee debenture issues by 301 (d) licenses in amounts dependent on the private capitalization of the licensee. Section 317 of the Act applied a reduced interest rate to the debentures purchased by the SBA during the first five years that each debenture is outstanding.

Since the intent of Congress, in authorizing sale of stock and debentures to MESBICs with subsidy, was to alleviate operating difficulties and lower the cost of capital, the preferred stock sold to the SBA should carry a flat dividend rate of 3 percent per annum, not a cumulative rate. Also, debentures sold to the SBA should receive an interest subsidy for the first five years of the term of the debentures with no obligations on the part of the licensee to pay the dividend or interest differential after the first five years when a distribution is made to stockholders other than the SBA.

The adoption of these new regulations should significantly assist in accomplishing the following: [33]

1. Encouraging the growth and expansion of MESBICs by attracting the private sector to invest more heavily in the MESBICs. A preferred security, which in effect penalizes distribution to stockholders other than the SBA, only detracts investors from MESBICs.
2. Increasing the marketability of preferred securities to individual investors other than the SBA.
3. Enabling MESBICs to determine the exact cost of preferred stock financing. Under the present system, MESBICs are unable to determine their cost of preferred stock because of uncertainties in payment schedules which are due to the discretionary power of the SBA to demand or not demand payment.
4. Giving MESBICs the necessary operating revenues, while at the same time offsetting any high debt servicing burden, especially in the early years.
5. Encouraging MESBICs to sell debentures to the SBA, thereby making more money available for small concerns and allowing them to expand and be more capable of operating profitably. This would enable them to achieve the goals of the MESBIC program.

There is no doubt that the MESBIC program's intent has been good from the very beginning. Economic advancement has proved the viability of the MESBIC as a vehicle for minority capitalism. The retail and services type industries have been more popular in the past than the emerging industries, such as transportation, mining, construction, and manufacturing. Nevertheless, with sufficient capital and management technical assistance in the proper industries, the MESBIC program should be able to achieve its social purpose.

4

Commercial Banking in the Inner Cities

Introduction and History

During Senate Committee hearings, as previously cited it was revealed that only about 10 percent of the Puerto Rican-American business firms had bank accounts and only 5 percent used any type of bank credit. Many of these firms had received their initial financing from loan sharks.[1] This is not a surprising revelation since up until recent times many minority businessmen could not find financial backing to buy equipment for expanding their operations. In an address given to the 79th annual convention of the Savings Bank Association of New York State, the executive director of the National Urban League, Vernon E. Jordan alleged that some of the savings and loan corporations and savings banks were participating in a planned disinvestment policy. His argument was based on the findings released by the Urban League on the lending practices of some of the major financial institutions located in predominantly Puerto Rican and Black neighborhoods in the Bronx area of New York. His allegations were that while these lending institutions had enjoyed increases in their assets and deposits, the institutions for the most part refused to grant new mortgages or provide refinancing at reasonable competitive rates.

This problem of financial resource misallocation was similarly acknowledged by the conservative U.S. Senator John Tower who stated:

> We have in America at any given time substantial amounts of unused and incompletely used capital, existing in banks, in corporations, and in Government, which can be more efficiently supplied to the market demand for capital, with increased effort by business and government.[2]

Frederick Sturdivant, in an empirical study of the activities of financial institutions in the East Los Angeles *barrio* concluded:

> While not as directly involved as auto dealers and other kinds of outlets in the "retail" structure of the community, financial institutions play a potentially significant role in East Los Angeles. As a potential source of consumer loans, these institutions could assist the residents of the area in avoiding many of the pitfalls associated with financing purchases through unethical merchants. In spite of the need, however, most of the financial institutions practice a rather conservative policy regarding loans to local residents.[3]

91

The following series of quotations[4] summarize the minority banker's view as to why it was necessary to organize indigenous institutions:

> Negroes must learn the philosophy of capitalism and how to develop revenue-producing communities. [Henry P. Hervey, President, Independent Bank of Chicago]

> In some banking institutions, the black businessman does not have the opportunity to present his ideas or loans because the black businessman is turned away by the loan officer simply because he is black. Other potential black businessmen are not able to present adequately prepared financial information and because there may be a communication barrier between the loan officer and the black businessman, many potential black businessmen never open businesses, or their businesses never grow beyond the owner-operated shop. [Edward E. Tillmon, Pres., Bank of Finance and NBA president]

> I don't believe that there should be any ownership of a Negro bank by a white institution. [L. Wilson York, Vice President and Cashier, First State Bank, Danville, Virginia]

> For years—funds have been going to banks who had little interest and no identification with the black community. [I.C. Squires, Pres., Swope Parkway National Bank]

The surfacing of minority lending institutions has come about by the inner city constituency attempting to provide minority-owned firms equal access to banking services for minorities and to provide a source of funds for capital formation and further economic growth for their communities. There are several reasons as to why minorities have played relatively modest roles in the banking industry. Most of them can be related to insufficiencies in capital, information, and labor.

The first problem is the inaccessibility to minorities of an adequate source of capital so as to develop internally and sustain a viable financial system. As Edward Irons, former executive Director of NBA, expressed:

> It is well known that absentee-owned banks and other industries operating in the black community do not reinvest their profits in the community. It is for this reason that I think these banks should be primarily black-owned.[5]

Another reason has been the general lack of information for planning and organizing a commercial bank. Next is the shortage of trained and experienced personnel. It is expected that by developing a group of minority financial institutions, that this will motivate ethnic groups to become entrepreneurs in other modestly represented areas of business. Another obstacle faced is that financial institutions entering into the activity for the first time face problems on two sides. One is a history of deprivation of wealth, skills, and experience and the other is the task of operating within the environment of the poor.

Adding greater dimension to the problem are the social expectations that minority banks should be simultaneously maximizing social welfare along with profits. When they receive their charters, it is implicitly understood that they should concentrate their banking services in the ghetto. After having examined the conditions under which inner city residents receive bank charters, there is every reason to believe that a charter would not be granted if a minority group contemplated establishing it outside the confines of their ethnic community. What this in effect sanctions is a separatist Jim Crow policy. With this restriction of their market area, minority banks are expected to be concerned with taking the lead in such issues as recruiting and training minorities, specializing in loans to minority-owned firms, providing mortgage financing for slum clearance, and to mobilize their resources so as to aid the war on poverty. Minority financial institutions are expected to assume the herculean task of correcting the economic injustices of the past. Past discrimination created the social problems confronted by minorities.

> It helped cement the ghetto walls. It helped insure inadequate ghetto schools.[6]

Minority lending institutions in general have a much more difficult task than do most new commercial banks. The impoverished clientele that characterizes inner cities markets makes it much more difficult to perform on a par with other institutions. Conditions of high unemployment and low income levels result in dissavings or marginal rates of savings. This takes its toll by making available meager resources thus making it possible to service only a small portion of the members of the inner cities.

A high concentration of small scale retail and service outlets limits both portfolio and product diversification. All these influences add to and reinforce the precarious nature of the environment.

Lending credence to this, is a statement which was made by the minority bank president, L.C. Squires at Swope Parkway National Bank, who stated that they

> Have not had the advantage of servicing large profitable businesses because there are only a few such businesses owned and operated by Black Americans in all of America. Therefore, banks owned and operated by Black Americans have been limited due to the social and economic conditions of their environment.[7]

Some observers consider the appearance of minority banks in recent years to be the birth of a new phenomenon—perhaps because the historic undertakings of minorities have often attracted little general attention. Actually, Black (or minority) banks can be traced back to the days of Reconstruction in the latter 1800s. Also, if it were possible to piece together the Vice-Royalty period of Spain and Mexico prior to the Treaty of Guadalupe-Hidalgo in 1848, we would probably find several banks owned by the Spanish-speaking population.

It is much easier to trace the history of Blacks in banking than of other minorities. After the Civil War, Black Union soldiers' funds in special military savings institutions provided the source of capital for starting the first depository institutions for the newly emancipated slaves. On March 3, 1865, the Freedman's Savings and Trust Company—usually referred to as Freedman Savings Bank—was sponsored by the Freeman's Bureau of Federal Government, and authorized by a decree of the U.S. Congress and the endorsement of President Lincoln.

The first chartered Black bank was established in the northern city of New York; later, it moved to Washington, D.C. During its heyday, Freedman's Savings and Trust maintained thirty-four to thirty-six branches, and accumulated $57 million in deposits distributed among the branches, 95 percent of which were located throughout the southern states.

Although this financial institution is historically cited as the first minority bank venture, it was, in fact, managed by White administrators, whose purpose was to create a depository for the savings of Blacks. Despite the efforts of Frederick Douglass to bolster confidence in the Freedman's Bank by extending a $10,000 loan from his personal savings and by assuming the responsibilities of bank president, the Bank lasted for only nine years. It failed because of the mismanagement by White administrators, and because of changes made by Congress in the Bank's investment policy.[8]

According to Gunnar Myrdal and the National Bankers Association (NBA),[a] the failure of Freedman's Bank severely weakened confidence in the viability of Black financial institutions. As a consequence, it was not until about fourteen years later that Blacks directly associated themselves with the banking field. In the year 1888, the first Black-owned bank was organized. It was chartered under the somewhat theological title of the Grand Foundation United Order of True Reformers in Richmond County, Virginia. The True Reformer Bank served as a depository for the Grand Order fraternal insurance company.

The True Reformer also ended in failure after operating for twenty years. However, during this time period, there were several new financial institutions that were started up by Blacks. From 1888 to 1934, approximately 134 financial firms were established by Blacks and were labeled "banks." Most of these institutions, however, functioned principally as depositories rather than as intermediaries. They provided a source of deposit protection for Black fraternal societies, charitable institutions, and churces. Many of these banks eventually

---

[a]The National Bankers Association is the minority equivalent of the American Bankers Association. It is the national trade association of minority-owned banks as was organized in 1927. At the time it was founded, the association was chartered under the name of the National Negro Bankers Association and represented a charter membership of twelve minority banks.

became insolvent. The problems they encountered which lead to their insolvency included overinvestment in assets with long-term maturities, overappraised real estate values, and a general lack of management training and experience. After 1908, the financial institutions that were organized by Blacks functioned more as intermediaries than as general depositories.

On the eve of the Bank Holiday of 1933, eleven Black banks remained in operation in five of the southern states.[b] Of these eleven banks, seven are still in existence. These banks are listed below in order of tenure and in accordance to geographical location.

Banking Institution	Date of Incorporation	Location
1. Consolidated Bank and Trust company	July 1903	Richmond, Virginia
2. Citizens Savings Bank and Trust Co.	January 1904	Nashville, Tennessee
3. Mechanics' and Farmers' Bank	March 1908	Durham, North Carolina
4. First State Bank and Trust Company	September 1919	Danville, Virginia
5. Citizens' Trust Company	June 1921	Atlanta, Georgia
6. Victory Savings Bank	October 1921	Columbia, South Carolina
7. Carver State Bank	January 1927	Savannah, Georgia

In 1934, the Industrial Bank of Washington, D.C. was established. After 1934, there was a period of dormancy in which no Blacks were granted either state or federal charters.

During the 1940s, three state charters were issued: to Tri-State Bank (1946) in Memphis, Tennessee; Carver Savings Bank (1947) in Savannah, Georgia; and Douglas State Bank (1947) in Kansas City, Kansas.

On December 31, 1960, the NBA announced that its membership had increased by one. The aggregate assets of these thirteen minority banking institu-

---

[b]Some of the Black banks that were on the verge of bankruptcy were acquired by Whites as a result of Blacks not being able to locate other Black interest or because bank regulatory agencies had authorized a forced sale due to the serious financial problems of these institutions. Recent examples of Black bank failure or acquisition by nonminorities are Crown Savings Bank, in Newport News, Virginia; Citizens and Southern in Philadelphia, Pennsylvania; and Farmers' State Bank in Boley, Oklahoma, which was the same town that experienced the failure of one of the few Black national banks. Crown Savings failed and was eventually closed in 1964. Citizens and Southern Bank was acquired by a nonminority control group in the late 1950s. The bank underwent several organizations since it became nonminority owned. Currently, it is operating under the name of the Centennial Bank. The Farmers' State Bank closed under voluntary liquidation in 1962.[9]

tions amounted to $58 million. In 1963, a national charter was granted to Riverside National Bank located in Houston, Texas. This was the third national charter to be granted to members of the Black community and the first to be issued in over forty years. It was also the first commercial bank to be organized by minorities in eighteen years.[c] The other two, the Douglas National Bank of Chicago, Illinois, and the Boley National Bank of Boley, Oklahoma, have failed since then.

By the end of 1963, there were ten minority lending institutions. Nine of these were operating under state charters, and one under a national charter. At this time, Blacks were the only members of a minority group who had made an inroad into the banking field. The Spanish-speaking and other minorities had not been able to establish themselves within the industry.

The end of 1963 marks the beginning of a new era in minority banking. This period is characterized by accelerated growth in the number of banking institutions. In contrast to their predecessors, most of the Black commercial banks which were chartered after 1963 have chosen to locate in northern or western states. Many of these were nationally chartered as a result of the U.S. Comptroller of the Currency adopting more liberal policies. Similarly, state-chartering agencies also adopted more liberal policies.

Although the decade of the 1960s showed a marked increase in the number of minority-owned financial institutions, deposit transfer was not as rapid. In 1967, a survey conducted by the Department of Economic Opportunity showed nonminorities still held 91.1 percent of the deposits of inner city residents. In 1969, there were twenty-two minority banks with assets totalling $259 million and total deposits amounting to $230 million. These aggregate figures represented 0.049 percent of the total assets and 0.053 percent of the total deposits of all insured commercial banks in the United States. This represented a fractional increase from the 0.019 percent and 0.020 percentage share which had prevailed during 1958. Although minority banks had doubled in number, they still represented a fraction of a fraction of the banking industry.

In June of 1970, their number was augmented to twenty-six, sixteen with state charters and ten with national. When the year ended the NBA had disclosed that minority depository institutions held assets of $338 million. The following year the number of minority banks had increased to thirty-five. This represented a 250 percent increase in number from the group that existed in 1962. Ten percent of these institutions had received national charters. By December 31, 1972, there were forty-one minority-owned commercial banks. From the group, thirty-four could be identified as Black-owned and the remaining seven as owned by members of other minority groups, mostly Mexican-Americans.

At this time, they held $676.9 million in assets and had total deposits of $596.3 million. This constituted a total industry asset and deposit share of

---

[c]An interesting feature concerning the organization of Riverside National Bank was that it was organized by the Executive Director of NBA, Edward D. Irons.

0.092 and 0.097 percent respectively. From 1958 to 1968, the asset growth rate for minority banks was 10 percent per year. The growth rate accelerated to 16 percent over the period from 1968 to 1972. If minority lending institutions continued to grow at the rapid pace of 16 percent, it would not be until A.D. 2020 that they would be able to acquire an asset share of the industry equal to *one* percent. If they were to slip back into the 10 percent growth path they experienced between 1958 and 1968, then it would be seventy-three years before minority banks would hold *one* percent of the banking assets in the United States. Although the number of minority banks has been rapidly increasing, this has not been sufficient to offset the relatively miniscule importance of their position in the commercial banking industry. In fact, while minority banks have been experiencing rapid growth so have other banks. For example if we compare the total assets of all minority banks in 1972 to the asset holding of Bank of America, we find that minorities accounted for less than 2 percent of this bank's assets.

By 1975, there were more than fifty minority or multiracially owned banks located throughout most parts of the United States. A Puerto Rican group had opened the Pan American National Bank in Union City, New Jersey. It opened with one of the largest capitalization figures for a minority bank, $1.5 million. During the year that Pan American was chartered in New Jersey, there were three additional national charters as well as two state charters granted to minorities. Among this group were the Atlantic National Bank in Norfolk, Virginia; Greensboro National Bank in Greensboro, North Carolina; Skyline National Bank in Denver, Colorado; Banco del Pueblo in Santa Ana, California; and North Milwaukee State Bank in Milwaukee, Wisconsin. The capitalization figure for the six banks totalled $5.5 million. From this group, five are still in operation. The lone fatality was the Skyline National Bank, which closed in March 1973.

Some of the new additions to the minority banking community are the Mexican-American National Bank in San Diego, California; Continental National Bank in Miami, Florida; United Southwest National Bank of Santa Fe in Santa Fe, Texas; National Bank of Brownsville in Brownsville, Texas; Pan American National Bank of Dallas in Dallas, Texas; Union National Bank of Austin in Austin, Texas; Continental Bank of El Paso in El Paso, Texas; First Prudential Bank of West Palm Beach in West Palm Beach, Florida; First Bank and Trust of Cleveland in Cleveland, Ohio; and the American Indian National Bank in Washington, D.C.[d] The current asset structure of the minority banking community is shown in Tables 4-1 and 4-2.

What we see in Table 4-1 is that with the exception of a few, most of the minority banks that have the largest asset holdings are those that received char-

---

[d]Another noteworthy bank is the multiracial Hemisphere National Bank, whose fifteen member board of directors has a two-thirds Spanish-speaking representation. Currently, there is an Asian-American group that is seeking a bank charter for operating in the District of Columbia. If and when this takes place, there will be a cross-sectional representation of most minority groups in the banking industry. Asian owned banks such as Sumitomo or the Bank of Tokyo are not recognized as minority banks because their ownership is principally

ters during the era of the 1960s. Half of these banks are organized under a national charter and the other half are organized under the state. These "new era banks" are larger and are growing at much faster rates than their predecessors. Most of them are located in major metropolitan areas where the competition is greater. The two largest banks are Independence Bank of Chicago and Seaway National Bank of Chicago, and both would come under the lower intermediate class category. Independence Bank of Chicago has $60.7 million in assets and Seaway Bank's total assets amounts to $48 million. Although they constitute 4 percent of the minority banks, their combined asset share represents 14 percent. This group with above average asset shares accounts for 79 percent of assets held by minority banks. The ten largest banks account for almost half of the assets. Of the twenty-six banks with greater than average asset holdings, most are Black-owned. The asset range is between $60 and $11 million dollars with the majority of the bank following within $10–$50 million dollar asset size.

In Table 4-2, most of the older banks are more closely clustered together in size. Whereas there was a $50 million range between the larger banks, there is only a $10 million range differential for the smaller institutions. Within this grouping, Unity State Bank of Dayton, Ohio, is the largest, with $10.5 million in total assets; and Pan American National Bank of Dallas, Texas, is the smallest with less than a one million dollar asset structure. In contrast, whereas the larger institution size difference can be attributed to operational or competitive strength, the size disparity shown between the smaller firms can in part be accounted to their embryonic state of development. Many are banks which have just received their charters and are just beginning to commence their operations.

Some of the older banks have not fared too well as compared to the younger institutions. There are examples where banks having ages of between two and four years have been able to outperform institutions that are fifty years their senior. The implication is that not only is it erroneous to group together the very young with the very old, but it is also misleading to think that the past performance of the older institutions is somehow a reflection of the future. A recent journalistic treatment of minority banks described them in the following manner:

> In recent years, the fashionable remedy for this [bank] prejudice has been the development of black banks that would get their deposits from and lend to the black community. Like so much else that has been fashionable in the last decade, this was a thoroughly stupid idea. The black businessmen, even more than the white businessman, wants to do his banking at a bank that can be helpful to him in establishing his credit with suppliers.

---

foreign. Both banks have 52 percent foreign membership. Besides, their size alone would raise questions about their comparative social disadvantage, since both individual banks have assets over $500 million. The minority bank classification also excludes two banks which are headquartered in Puerto Rico with branches in the United States.

Table 4-1

Asset Structure of the Minority Banks with Above Average Asset Holdings

Minority Commercial Banks	Total Assets (in millions of dollars)	Percentage of Total	Cumulative Percentage
Independence Bank of Chicago Chicago, Illinois (1964)	$60.692	7.81%	7.81%
Seaway National Bank of Chicago Chicago, Illinois (1965)	48.114	6.19	14.00
Industrial Bank of Washington Washington, D.C. (1934)	41.208	5.30	19.30
Mechanics and Farmers Bank Durham, North Carolina (1907)	38.022	5.01	24.31
Freedom National Bank New York, New York (1964)	36.787	4.73	29.04
First Independence National Bank Detroit, Michigan (1970)	31.749	4.00	33.12
International Bank of Commerce of Laredo Laredo, Texas (1966)	30.178	3.88	37.00
Bank of Finance Los Angeles, California (1964)	29.827	3.84	40.84
United National Bank of Washington, D.C. Washington, D.C. (1964)	26.097	3.40	44.20
Tri-State Bank of Memphis Memphis, Tennessee (1946)	23.468	3.00	47.22
The Douglas State Bank Kansas City, Missouri (1947)	23.468	2.50	49.76
South Side Bank Chicago, Illinois (1973)	19.566	2.52	52.28
First Enterprise Bank Oakland, California (1972)	19.180	2.40	54.75
Gateway National Bank St. Louis, Missouri (1965)	18.704	2.41	57.16
Pan American National Bank Los Angeles, California (1965)	18.393	2.37	59.53
Highland Community Bank Chicago, Illinois (1970)	18.316	2.36	61.89
Gateway National Bank of Chicago Chicago, Illinois (1972)	16.985	2.00	64.07
Midwest National Bank Indianapolis, Indiana (1972)	15.450	1.99	66.06
First Plymouth National Bank Minneapolis, Minnesota (1969)	15.309	1.97	68.03
Pan American National Bank Union City, New Jersey (1971)	13.192	1.70	69.73
Riverside National Bank Houston, Texas (1962)	12.663	1.60	71.36
Liberty Bank and Trust Company New Orleans, Louisiana (1972)	12.543	1.61	72.97
Unity Bank and Trust Company Roxbury, Massachusetts (1968)	12.220	1.57	74.54
City National Bank of New Jersey Newark, New Jersey (1973)	11.747	1.50	76.04
Vanguard National Bank Hempstead, New York (1972)	11.452	1.47	77.51
First Bank and Trust of Cleveland Cleveland, Ohio (1974)	11.306	1.45	78.96

Source: Federal Deposit Insurance Corporation, 1975.

Table 4–2
Asset Structure of the Minority Banks with Below Average Asset Holdings

Minority Commercial Banks	Total Assets (in millions of dollars)	Percentage of Total	Cumulative Percentage
Unity State Bank Dayton, Ohio (1970)	$10.537	1.36%	80.52%
Pan American National Bank Houston, Texas (1970)	10.529	1.35	81.67
Carver State Bank Savannah, Georgia (1927)	10.299	1.32	82.99
Guaranty Bank and Trust Company Chicago, Illinois (1972)	10.218	1.31	84.30
Continental National Bank of Miami Miami, Florida (1974)	9.743	1.25	85.55
Centinel Bank of Taos Taos, New Mexico (1969)	9.638	1.24	86.79
Citizens Savings Bank and Trust Company Nashville, Tennessee (1904)	9.355	1.20	87.99
North Milwaukee State Bank Milwaukee, Wisconsin (1971)	9.159	1.18	89.17
Liberty Bank of Seattle Seattle, Washington (1969)	9.131	1.17	90.34
First State Bank Danville, Virginia (1919)	8.957	1.15	91.49
Atlantic National Bank Norfolk, Virginia (1971)	7.665	0.99	92.48
Banco del Pueblo Santa Ana, California (1971)	7.182	0.92	93.40
Peoples National Bank of Springfield Springfield, Illinois (1970)	5.885	0.76	94.16
Victory Savings Bank Columbia, South Carolina (1921)	5.792	0.74	94.90
Greensboro National Bank Greensboro, North Carolina (1921)	5.358	0.69	95.59
First Prudential Bank of West Palm Beach West Palm Beach, Florida (1974)	5.061	0.65	96.24
Pacific Coast Bank San Diego, California (1971)	4.944	0.64	96.88
Mexican American National Bank San Diego, California (1973)	4.879	0.63	97.51
American State Bank Tulsa, Oklahoma (1970)	4.858	0.62	98.13
Freedom Bank of Finance Portland, Oregon (1969)	4.771	0.61	98.74
Medical Centre State Bank Oklahoma City, Oklahoma (1973)	4.000	0.51	99.24
Community Bank of Nebraska Omaha, Nebraska (1973)	3.294	0.42	99.67
Brownsville National Bank Brownsville, Texas (1974)	1.000	0.13	99.80
Continental National Bank El Paso, Texas (1974)	1.000	0.13	99.93
Union National Bank[a] Austin, Texas	0.900	0.12	100.05
Pan American National Bank Dallas, Texas (1974)	0.750	0.10	100.15[b]

[a]In process of organization.
[b]Cumulative percentage adds up to more than 100% because of rounding errors.
Source: Federal Deposit Insurance Corporation 1975.

The better established the black business, the more prominent the bank with which it can develop a relationship. Thus the new black bank cannot hope to draw any significant business from the best part of its presumed market, which will be depositing and borrowing elsewhere. But it can get all the risky business it will take.[10]

What this emotive inference suffers from is the fallacy of temporal composition. The writer obviously assumed that his limited assessment of the past will apply equally to the future as well. Judging from the performance of the newer institutions, it is clear that "lump-sum analysis" of minority banks can at best leave us with just enough information to keep us misinformed.

It is hard to understand how the efforts to ensure intracommunity financial intermediation can be perceived as an act of stupidity. Furthermore, most of the evidence indicates that minorities prefer to do business with their own kind because of the assurance that elements of discrimination do not enter into the transaction.

As we black bankers put it, white banks often find it difficult to understand "the economics of low-income, minority communities."[11]

Another source states:

When there's a borderline case, a white company might say "Why fool with it," but a Negro officer would examine it to see if he could make the loan.[12]

Further, in terms of the cost of borrowing, as the previous president of the first minority bank in the state of California, Nivelle Beaubien, said:

Caucasian companies would make loans, but charge a higher rate. That's why we opened the bank.[13]

Granted, there may be a group of "better established black businesses" which prefer to bank with the nonminority sector, but as the Bureau of the Census disclosed, this segment represents less than one percent of the minority-owned businesses. What Martin Mayer is evidently advocating is to enshrine the status quo. Alas, the pharisaical views of this individual at best only serve to reinforce the myopic views of those who would fallaciously argue that economic and social parity were established with the Emancipation Proclamation.

Banking and the American Indian

The American Indian National Bank is headed by Mr. W.W. Keeler, former chief executive of Phillips Petroleum and Chairman of the President's Advisory

Council in Minority Business Enterprise. Mr. Keeler, who serves as Chairman of the Board is a Cherokee Indian. The Bank's president is Barney Old Coyote, a member of the Crow tribe.

The American Indian National Bank was organized to provide nationwide banking services to Indians, and to improve interethnic financial intermediation.[e] As stated by its President,

> A large portion of Indian money is spread across the country in many banks. This increases the operating and lending capacity of these banks, but does not increase the borrowing capacity of the Indians, nor does it provide them full access to all areas of financial services. It is the goal of this bank to progressively change that situation.[14]

Since the opening of the American Indian National Bank in November 1973, it has experienced a steady growth in deposits at a rate of about one million dollars per month, and one of its first loans was made to a chief from the Oklahoma Creek Indians, who received $375,000. This was the first time in the history of the United States that an Indian lending institution made a loan to a fellow Indian. This is seen as a significant economic advancement, since as one representative of the Mohawk-Iroquois from the Caughnawaga Reservation cited,

> One of the reasons why so many Indians are so poor and live in miserable shacks for which they are unjustly ridiculed: "Until just recently, Indians were not allowed mortgages. Banks could not lend them money because they could not foreclose on Indian property."[15]

In the past, in order for American Indians to obtain collateralized bank financing, they have had to rely on tribal funds, more commonly referred to as "band funds."

> Scant security, the difficulty of collection, and a lack of knowledge stood between the reservation Indians and the loan departments of commercial banks for years.[16]

An official from the American Indian National Bank stated that by 1975, the Bank's deposits should have grown to $20 million. Much of this rapid deposit growth has been credited to an aggressive deposit promotion aimed at selling the *raison-d'etre* to tribal officials. For example, the board chairman is cited as having visited the leaders of tribal councils of almost every major Indian nation and

---

[e]When the bank was organized, it restricted public stock holdings to American Indians or to people who could verify direct involvement with Indian programs. This restriction in the offering of common stock exceeded the requirements of the U.S. Treasury Department, which stipulates that only a minimum of 50 percent of equity outstanding must be owned by members of a minority population in order for a bank to be identified as minority-owned.

tribe in the United States in an effort to persuade them to deposit their funds with the Bank. Tribal councils have historically deposited their funds with the U.S. Treasury Department. An individual member of a tribe who would be seeking a loan would then have to appeal to the tribal council.

It was estimated by one of the Bank's senior vice presidents, Mr. Charles Swallow, that if they could obtain at least 10 percent of all tribal funds, they would be able to enjoy the position of a large bank.

In Montana, where the Department of Commerce estimates that Crow Indians have deposited between $1 and $1.5 million in state banks, an unusual type of partnership has been arranged between the Crow Indian Tribe and organizers of three new state-chartered banks. The Crow Indians have negotiated to assume 20 percent of the equity, or approximately $100,000 ownership share of each of the banks. The three banks are the Western State Bank and Western Bank, both in Billings, Montana, and the Western Bank of Bozeman.

The Crow Indians have been assured that job opportunities would be made available within the banks. Each commercial bank agreed to have at least one or more Indian bank officer trainees, and granted the Crows the right to nominate a tribal member to each board of directors. Thus, the Crow Indians have partly insured the outcome by holding directorships in the banks.

It was agreed that the preparatory training program for loan officers would last from six months to one year before an individual would begin on-the-job training. On-the-job training would take place in conjunction with evening courses at local chapters of the American Institute of Banking. By the end of two years, the average trainee would be on even ground with the typical bank employee.

The long-range plan of the Crow Indians is eventually to form their own financial institutions and tap the experience of the tribal bank directors and management trainees. In the meantime, their development strategy should insure that the flow of financial resources remains within the community of the Crow Indians and provides the financial means for underwriting economic growth.

The development strategy is intended to complement the appeal by the industrial development director for the National Congress of American Indians, for commercial banks to finance industrialization on Indian reservation.

One bank that has in the past been actively involved in providing installment financing to Indians has been Valley National Bank in Arizona. One bank loan officer estimates that 65 percent of these transactions are being channeled through Valley National. Every one of the state's fourteen Indian tribes is currently conducting business with the bank. Valley National has introduced a tribal guarantee loan program. The program allows the bank to make loans to Indians who would not qualify under Federal Reserve regulations because of insufficient collateral. The arrangement that has been worked out is a type of "compensating balance." Security is provided in the form of certificates of deposit that are issued to the respective tribe by the bank and correspond to the funds deposited with Valley National. The average annual interest rate in the early 1960s was 3 percent.

Polemics and Minority Banks

This section will be devoted to examining the controversy that surrounds the performance of the financial activities of minority commercial banks.

There has been much discussion in the literature as to whether minority lending institutions either facilitate or hinder economic growth in the inner city. Few would argue against the proposition that commercial banks occupy a pivotal position in the inter and intra flow of funds within a community. First, they can provide a means for transferring purchasing power claims from savers to investors. Secondly, they can supply a source of credit to local government, households, and firms. Where the disagreement seems to center is around the issues of whether the influence of these institutions has a direct or indirect effect on economic growth, or whether their influence depresses or stimulates economic development. "Direct" means is the sense that it causes growth in output and real capital formation, and "indirect" means that its appreciable effects register themselves in altering the entrepreneural spirit of a community. The latter could be viewed as part of human resource development, as a source of racial pride such as ornamental "badges of honor" symbolizing social accomplishment. Both of the questions have not been lacking in debate.[f] Much of the controversy began with Andrew Brimmer's presentation at the 1970 American Finance Association Meetings, where he disclosed that his cross-sectional study on "The Black Banks: An Assessment of Performance and Prospects," had evidence indicating that

> From this assessment of the performance of black banks, I am convinced that the multiplication of institutions should not be encouraged in the belief that they can make a major contribution to the financing of economic development of the black community.[17]

There are probably several people who are in disagreement with Brimmer's position that would find themselves in full accord with the above statement; certainly this would be true if twenty-two minority institutions are quixotically

---

[f]See, for example, the seminal discussion by Andrew Brimmer, "The Black Banks: An Assessment of Performance and Prospects," *op. cit.*, pp. 379–405; Edward Irons, "Black Banking: Problems and Prospects," *Journal of Finance,* Vol. 26 (May 1971), pp. 407–425; Mauris Emeka, "Some Common Problems of Black Banks in 1972," *The Review of Black Political Economy,* Vol. 3, No. 3 (Spring 1973), pp. 100–114; the comprehensive study by Jack Boorman, *New Minority-Owned Commercial Banks, A Comparative Analysis, op. cit.;* David L. Kohn, "Minority Owned Banks," *Federal Reserve Bank of Kansas City Monthly Review,* February 1972, pp. 11–20; J. R. Dominguez, "Capital Flows In Minority Communities," *The Review of Black Political Economy,* Vol. 5, No. 2 (Winter 1975), pp. 158–174.

viewed as being capable of correcting a legacy of poverty and enhancing the per capita incomes of a population of 22.7 Blacks. This is unquestionably, unadulterated wishful thinking. Banking authorities usually observe a rule of thumb that a commercial bank can adequately provide banking services to a population size of 7,500. If this is a correct estimate, then how can the average minority bank be expected to service one million members of its population. The demands are too great for too small a group. Most would agree that it is ludicrous to expect that a handful of minority banks can correct the institutionalized problem of income and wealth inequalities, especially when their relative share is 6.3 percent and 1.9 percent respectively as Brimmer shows in his "memorandum."[18]

Secondly, why should minority institutions be expected to be the financial caretakers of the poor? Particularly when the relative size of their resources is much more limited and much scarcer than that of the nonminority banking sector. This rationale is based on the accepted belief that social accountability should reside exclusively with minorities *ipso facto*. It is as though minorities arrived on the economic scene bringing and self-imposing their social ills upon themselves and, because of this, they should be held chiefly responsible for correcting their own misfortune.

Brimmer's remarks were in order, but for the wrong reasons. Minorities should not be obliged or be expected to undertake the lion's-share of the effort nor should they be expected to create silk purses out of sow's ears. The actual statement which most people took issue with was his closing comment that:

> Because of this combination of handicaps, the black banks as a group appear to possess very little potential as instruments of urban economic development.[19]

Brimmer's inference, however, leaves us with a directionless critique. He neither identifies nor does he establish what would be desirable properties of an "instrument of urban economic development." There are several serious problems with his conclusion. First of all, the analysis never does link the financial variables with measures of economic development. No evidence is presented showing how the minority banking structure has or has not affected aggregate indicators of development such as minorities' real gross or net product, output and employment diversification, per capita income, income distribution, changes in social overhead, output per head of the labor force, output per man hour, changes in the capital stock or the rate of capital formation, human resource development, increases in the supply of skilled labor, and changes in employment or unemployment, which are but a few of the economic variables Brimmer could have examined.

Furthermore, he makes no mention of possible changes in capital formation which could be brought about from residential and consumer loans via the acceleration principle or changes in aggregate minority income which could be brought about from expansionary multiplier effects. This is particularly relevant when consideration is given to the high marginal propensity to consume that characterize minority communities.

Instead, the analysis reduces to a single period cross-sectional comparison of loan-deposit ratios and the asset portfolio mix of minority banks *vis à vis* the rest of the federally insured banking industry. It is surprising that he should draw conclusions that have dynamic implications from a static sample. Brimmer examined the aggregate behavior of twenty-two inner cities based banks. From the consolidated data, he constructed average operating ratios for his sample, and he compared these inner cities bank averages to a composite industry average for all federally insured commercial banks. His general sources of information were consolidated reports of conditions and examination reports released by either the Comptroller of the Currency, Federal Reserve Board, or the Federal Deposit Insurance Corporation. Deposit size and Federal Reserve membership were the criteria for grouping and ranking minority banks.

The trouble with Brimmer's test sample is that he lumps together institutions of different vintages and treats the average of their behavior as though it were a cross-sectional representation of a prototype. With respect to the vintage discrepancy within Brimmer's sample, 32 percent of the banks are over the age of forty years and 55 percent had been operating for six years or less. As a consequence, 87 percent of his sample was made up of the very young and the very old. Only two minority banks cluster around the average sample age of twenty-two years. By lumping together junior banks with senior institutions and measuring the average of their behavior, the erroneous impression is given that what is being observed is the performance of the mature bank. This is obviously misleading. Furthermore, the average age for the group over forty was fifty-two years and for the group of six years or under, the average age was three years. To draw behavioral conclusions from a sample with this type of age dispersal is analogous to interpreting the intelligence quotient scores of children of elementary school age and those of people over the age of fifty in such a manner that one is led to believe that what is being measured is the performance level of an individual in his early twenties.

This study also suffers from the problem of drawing a comparison between apples and pears. At *no* time are comparative performance measures applied to nonminority banks having equal size and competing in the same market. Since Brimmer chose to analyze only minority-owned banks performance in the inner cities, we cannot know whether his conclusion that minority banks possess little potential as instruments of urban economic development is not equally true of nonminority banks operating in minority areas.

Brimmer inferred from his findings that minority-owned or minority-controlled commercial banks should not be encouraged in the belief that they have significant impact on the inner city because minority banks for the most part, aside from being high cost-low profit operations, are overly conservative in their lending, have a hoarding tendency towards excess liquid balances, are net exporters of capital, and prefer to invest in short-term governmental securities and real estate. Understandably, Brimmer's research conclusions have not been favorably received among business development organizations and minority bankers who see minority banks as the means for "providing minority-owned businesses equal access to banking services, and becoming an increasingly important source of capital for minority enterprise and community growth."[20]

In the 1972 gathering of the National Bankers Association, a paper was presented entitled "Asset Management in a Profit Oriented Black Bank." The thrust of the paper was "to make a case for all minority-owned banks in the country as a group, as a positive force in the nation's economy."[21] This paper demonstrated that although two years had passed since Brimmer had presented his polemical findings, the controversy still lingered. Brimmer's work can be brought to task for its failure to distinguish between hoarding and the maintenance of a liquidity posture that is necessary in order to handle the greater deposit turnover characteristic of minority communities. Additionally, Brimmer can be criticized for failing to distinguish between the different types of reserve commitments associated with deposits. For example, as a result of the U.S. government's Deposit Solicitation Program, minority banks have a large percentage of collateralized deposits that must be matched with a pledge of eligible securities. This explains why inner cities lending institutions have a lower loan-to-deposit ratio and a high government securities portfolio. Moreover, an exercised caution in lending may not in practice reflect the risk aversion of the lenders but rather the governing concerns of the regulators.

A more fundamental problem in Brimmer's analysis is its static nature. While under normal circumstances, ratio analysis may give a reasonably good perspective of a commercial bank's operation, it is incomplete in one important respect—it ignores the dimension of time. Brimmer's ratios represent a minority bank's position at one point in time, rather than showing behavior trends. Similarly, he presumes these stationary values can also serve as a preview of the future. This is somehow expecting too much uniformity within the movement of time. In the sixth century B.C., the Greek philosopher Heraclitus noted that all observable phenomena were in flux, and "the only thing constant is change." Given this maxim, it is highly unlikely that minority banks would be an exception to this Athenian observation.

Brimmer discusses capital outflows emanating from minority financial institutions, yet he fails to disclose in what direction these flows are moving over time. An analysis of ratios over a time interval may reveal a decline in the observed financial condition or a reversal.

Brimmer's sample ratios have additional biases, particularly in the case of economies of scale. For example, larger commercial banks can perform a wider range of services that may help to minimize their operating costs, such as providing specialized personnel to manage security portfolios, evaluate credit and loans, and perform trust operations. Since minority banks are "about one-third the size of the typical bank in the country at large," in comparing the aggregate costs and asset (or deposit) structures of minority and nonminority banks, we should expect them to differ because of this size difference.

The degree of risk associated with operating on a small scale is another disadvantage faced by the smaller bank, and is therefore a potential cause of bias which relates to size rather than racial attributes.

> Particularly, the liklihood is great that an expansion in scale tends to result in a decline in risks, since a larger portfolio of loans permits a greater degree of portfolio diversification, and hence a reduction in the degree of uncertainty with respect to losses. Lending operations are more efficient on a larger scale for reasons associated with principles of insurance.[22]

Finally, what can be said in summary is that too much was concluded from too little evidence and that this study is subject to the same type of myopia metaphorically mirrored in Plato's *Allegory of the Cave*. The conclusion that we can draw from Brimmer's seminal study is that there is insufficient evidence to substantiate the charge that minority banks possess little potential as instruments of urban economic development.

5

Capital Flows and the Economics of the Inner Cities

Introduction

In recent years the issue of developing the inner city has gained considerable attention. This is largely due to a general awareness that the economic development of minorities has not progressed at an even pace with the advancement of other Americans.

Before discussing the economic attributes of the inner city, it is necessary to build a conceptual framework for understanding the flows of resources and the behavior of economic units inside and outside of the inner city. For purposes of delineating the inner city sector, it is useful to view it as an underdeveloped enclave. Economic units that exist inside and outside of the inner city are business firms owned by both minorities and nonminorities. Economic units outside have enjoyed benefits from minorities. These benefits have been the supply of low cost labor and capital to nonminority households and firms, as well as the receipts from inner city residents' consumption expenditures.

Households and firms within minority areas interact in six transaction domains: (1) consumption goods and services supplied by small minority-owned firms, (2) consumption goods and services supplied by nonminority-owned firms operating in the inner city, (3) consumption goods and services supplied by firms from the rest of the economy, (4) resource or factor markets of minority-owned firms located in the inner city, (5) resource or factor markets of nonminority-owned firms in the ghetto, and (6) resource or factor market firms emanating from the rest of the economy.

Within these six areas of transactions, minority households furnish mainly semiskilled and unskilled labor to minority-owned firms that are primarily engaged in the services and retail trade industries, in exchange for money wages. This exchange between minority households and minority-owned firms represents the supply and demand in the minority-owned factor markets.[1]

In contrast, households outside of the inner cities supply nonminority-owned ghetto firms with nonminority capital and nonminority labor. In addition, there is a modest minority labor supply that satisfies the demands of nonminority sectors. The pecuniary benefits to nonminority households from the offering of their factor services include rents, interest, wages, salaries, etc.

On the demand side, goods and services produced by nonminority-owned firms located in the inner city are consumed mostly by inner city residents.

109

The converse is, for the most part, not true. Nonminority households do not on the whole consume goods produced by minority-owned firms based in or out of the inner city. Consequently, this gives rise to a steady outflow of capital, assuming that the nonminority firm does not reinvest all its earnings back into the inner city. This outflow is compounded by the practice of inner city residents consuming mostly goods and services that originate outside their community. Thus, the minority community has little capital available for expanding or diversifying its production base. The interactive economic and financial flows that take place between the nonminority community at large and the inner city are illustrated in Figure 5-1.

Ghetto Development Strategies

Since the urban riots of the 1960s, many development approaches have been suggested both by public agents and by private organizations for what the Kerner Commission euphemized as "ghetto enrichment." These strategies have ranged from Black Capitalism to the GHEDIPLAN[2] (Ghetto Economic Development and Industrialization Plan) to the Community Development Corporations. Two other related strategies that merit mentioning are the establishment of branch plant facilities in the inner city—some wholly owned by nonminorities and others organized as joint ventures[a]—and the federally operated public sector central cities programs. The largest and most publicized of these programs have been the Demonstration Cities, the Model Cities Program, and the program created by the Metropolitan Development Act of 1966. The latter was enacted by the U.S. Congress. The program entailed a five-year appropriation to provde noncategorical funds to municipalities and city governments to be allocated for the purpose of "breaking the poverty cycle" in "model neighborhoods." The grants are aimed at this end. After the U.S. Department of Housing and Urban Development screens the application, the funds are then administered by a "city demonstration agency," a division of City Hall which is authorized to act as the planning institution for the inner city.

Distinctions have been made between the strategies of "Black Capitalism" and community development. The first concept is associated with the goal of widespread development of atomistic firms, under the current conventional institutions. The second idea centers on the formal organization of economic development units, which implies the active support of governmental agencies and inner cities' producers and consumers, all acting in unison with common social goals. Within this approach, profits are relegated to a secondary station.

---

[a]In some of these projects, "turnkey" arrangements have been made by which ownership of the plant would eventually be transferred either to a community group or to a minority entrepreneur, after the venture was successfully underway.

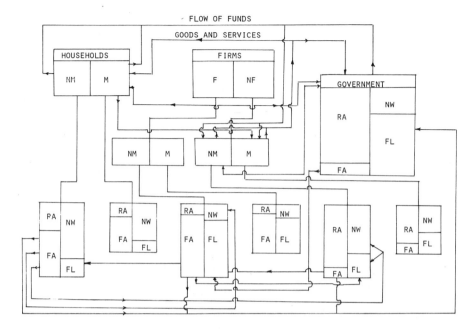

Figure 5-1. Product and Resource Flow for the U.S. Economy.
RA, real assets; FA, financial assets; NW, net worth; FL, financial
liabilities; NM, nonminority; M, minority; H, household; F, financial;
NF, nonfinancial; BF, business firms; G, government.

The following is a review of the recent attempts to reshape the economic
structure of the inner city. This will include the orthodox approaches of Black
Capitalism, corporate relocation, the Model Cities program, and organized community development. ("Orthodox" means in the sense that they involve only
minimal institutional change, and do not transfer resource control power to
minority organizations.)[3]

Black Capitalism

The term "Black Capitalism" first appeared in public discussion in 1968
when Richard Nixon adopted it as a slogan to represent the Administration's
interest in the development of minority entrepreneurship. To some extent the
term is misleading, because it has a connotation directed towards the Blacks, to
the exclusion of other minorities.

The following definition of "Black Capitalism" by Theodore Cross probably
best exemplifies its directional aims:

Black Capitalism is the strategy which urges creation of new jobs and profit centers inside ghetto areas. The program also seeks to transfer the ownership of ghetto business from white to black control, at the same time building in the ghetto new banks, insurance companies, production and service facilities.[4]

The problem with the aims of this definition is that Black Capitalism is seen solely as a ghetto transfer of business title without a provision for altering the allocative capital mechanism or for correcting institutional elements of discrimination. Yet, many would argue that indigenous ownership of business enterprises in the inner cities is the first step that must be taken for eradicating the injustices of poverty, and for creating conditions conducive to economic integration.

The term "Black Capitalism" has also been used to mean mobilization of both private and public resources, aimed at expanding the scope of minority business participation. Historically, it has been common practice for minority groups to be excluded from ownership of businesses within their own communities. For example, four-fifths of Black-owned establishments in Harlem in the winter of 1967–68 were controlled by nonminorities.[5] Nonminority-owned firms in the Harlem ghetto were also significantly more profitable than Black enterprises, as revealed by a study of tax returns in 1968.[6] Thus, the aims of Black Capitalism are to reduce absentee ownership and "give minorities a bigger piece of the action."

Other positive externalities would be the improvement of consumer welfare in the inner city and the creation of conditions conducive to larger and more efficiently operated firms, where economies of scale provide lower prices and higher quality merchandise.

Finally, proponents of Black Capitalism hope that indigenous ownership will bring about social stability in the inner city. Nonminority absentee ownership of a large number of firms in minority communities has been a major cause of social unrest.[7] Conflicts with nonminority merchants occur frequently. As mentioned previously, the Kerner Commission found that these conflicts constituted one of the sparks which ignited the Watts riots.

One critic of the notion of Black Capitalism has been Andrew Brimmer, who has argued that investment in the inner cities is inefficient and therefore socially wasteful, given the unfavorable economic climate of minority communities and the omnipresence of crime.[8] A parallel argument has been made that low marginal efficiency of investment in minority ghettos is a sufficient reason to discontinue subsidies.

In response to these criticisms, one can say that the unfavorable economic climate in the ghettos is largely a result of a history of underinvestment in the capital formation of the ghetto.[9] Capital investment and technological improvements in the inner city economy will improve the "climate." For certain, unsubsidized private investment has not come forth, nor is it likely to be forth-coming from the suasion of the "invisible hand." Regarding the prevalence of crime, it is evident that whenever poverty is matched with high levels of social and economic aspiration, the environmental setting is conducive to crime. This is especially true for criminal acts against person and property, which involve a forcible transfer of purchasing power. When people are prevented from obtaining desired social and economic goals legally, they will seek to acquire them illegally.

> Thus we find that ghettos of large cities produce a disproportionate share of criminals. The incidence of robbery and traffic in illegal goods tends to be high among minority groups who feel the burden of both economic and social discrimination.[10]

As an alternative to the described policies of assistance to minority entre-preneurs, Brimmer advocates employing human capital development programs.[b] Underlying his argument is the belief that well-educated, trained minority work-ers will have the potential to be attracted to business firms with higher expected returns and greater job security. While this may be true in frictionless markets that are untainted by discriminatory hiring practices, the issue still remains that there is *no* assurance that workers will be hired in the first place, and secondly, that, if they were hired, they would enjoy any upward mobility within non-minority organizations.

Supporters of Black Capitalism assert that minority ownership would change the flow of receipts payments in favor of those living inside the minority community. The inner city would receive a greater volume of rents, interests, wages, and salaries, and would be less dependent on wages and salaries as its principal source of income. Other direct benefits would be career direction for inner city youth. According to Roy F. Lee,

> Thus one of the side benefits of movements such as black capitalism is that the minority youth who will crystallize his final choice in a decade or so will have businessmen as models; and he will at the time of his choice, see at least some opportunities.[11]

Although most appraisals of Black Capitalism during the 1960s seem to center on the negative, there is one observer who is not in agreement.

> Despite a myriad of adverse conditions, a small black business community has stubbornly managed to survive; because capital was extremely scarce, the overwhelming majority of black entrepreneurs concentrated in lines of business requiring little capital. When capital markets finally open up,

---

[b]In most of the literature on minority economic development one notes almost a universal preoccupation with the labor input, while the other production inputs, capital, land, and technology go untended.

black businesses will expand into fields in which they heretofore had been unable to compete on an equal basis . . . the SBA program opening capital markets for black entrepreneurs gives them an excellent opportunity for creating new firms and expanding existing ones.[12]

Location of Corporate Branch Plants in the Inner Cities

A group of U.S. Congressmen, under the leadership of the late Senator Robert F. Kennedy, advocated giving federal support to major corporations which located branch plants within the inner city.[13] The philosophy behind this effort was that the plants would create jobs and generate income, both directly and indirectly. Management could expect the new plants to stimulate the sales of adjacent small firms and also promote the development of both "line" workers and managers. Management also hoped that the "turnkey" programs, by which they set up subsidiaries to be taken over eventually by minority entrepreneurs, would enable inner city residents to participate in the earnings.

The major investments by these corporations were, however, short-lived, lasting from 1966 through 1970; since that time there have been no new investments under the auspices of this program realized in the inner city. At least part of the reason for the reluctance to continue investing in the minority communities was that over the trial period profit margins proved to be smaller than in other outside locations. No consideration has been given to the fact that the profit gestation period may be longer, and if this is true then a more lengthy investment horizon needs to be observed or supplementary tax and subsidy incentives need to be provided during the development stage of the branch plants, without such government support efforts voluntary corporate plant relocation will most likely remain minimal.

The success of branch-plant programs and the "turnkey" operation has not, in fact, been very spectacular. Many plants have closed down, as have turnkey operations. For example, by May 1969, the highly-publicized Watts Manufacturing Company had experienced substantial losses and had reduced the size of its work force considerably, in spite of Labor and Defense Department subsidies and contracts totaling well over $4 million.

Another program supported by the late Robert F. Kennedy, involved legislation designed to subsidize nonminority corporate branching. The plan continues to receive widespread attention from advocates of inner city economic development. The plan, which would have provided investment credits, accelerated depreciation allowances, wage subsidies, and training allowances, was subject to a corporation meeting certain conditions with respect to hiring of inner city residents. The one drawback of such a plan is that it may often attract firms operating closest to the loss margin, as they are the most responsive to these types of incentives.

In order to eliminate this drawback and attract more efficient corporations, measures have been suggested to change the factors to corporate viability and community needs. The plan suggested by Kennedy, however, made no provision for public investment in urban infrastructure, which is an integral part of economic development.

The Model Cities Program

In 1966, the U.S. Department of Housing and Urban Development undertook a Model Cities Program under Title I of the Metropolitan Development Act of 1966.[14] This program was designed to address itself to the grievances of social, economic, and physical problems of ghetto residents. A period of five years was proposed for upgrading the total environment of the inner city and improving the quality of life of the residents. Cities participating in the program received one year "planning grants" to carry out their programs.

To date, only a fraction of the Model Cities Program's budget has been allocated to activities that could be classified as related to economic development. Such activities would have included creation and support of new private and public ventures or construction of new additional housing. Indeed the inability to generate much construction or rehabilitation business for minority contractors has probably been the primary shortcoming of this program. Instead the program is primarily concerned with the delivery of services and the offering of direct public service employment via manpower training. Even with respect to the latter, only about 20 percent of the regular salaried, Model Cities-funded workers, in the spring of 1971, were employed in development related activities according to an unpublished HUD-commissioned study by the National Civil Service League.

Though the Model Cities program itself has recorded limited success, it has succeeded in establishing one of the few new governing institutions in American cities devoted to ameliorating the problems of the poor.

Economic Development

The decade of the 1960s witnessed the launching of a mixture of economic and social programs aimed specifically at affecting the economic development of the inner cities. The most visible and publicized effort was the development strategy of Black Capitalism. Other programs have either directly or indirectly attempted to complement the efforts of exporting capitalism to the minority communities. These have included manpower training and community development projects. The content and objectives of these programs have been to increase minority income and return on human capital. This section examines

trends in minority income, employment, and wealth in order to determine and
assess the social benefits of these recent strategies for inner city economic
development. Special emphasis is given to the economic status of the barrio residents of East Los Angeles, a 6.64 square mile area in metropolitan Los Angeles
which has a predominantly Mexican-American population that is currently
approaching a 90 percent density.

Table 5-1 shows trends in employment for both Blacks and Mexican-
Americans. From 1960 through 1969, the Black labor force rose in line with the
total civilian labor force; however, the participation rate (e.g., total labor force
as a percentage of the noninstitutionalized population) of Blacks declined increasingly.[15]

Between 1960 and 1969, total civilian employment increased by 18 percent
from 65.8 million in 1960 to 77.9 million in 1969. During this same period
employment of Blacks and nonminorities increased by 21 and 15 percent,
respectively. The Spanish-speaking minority showed an increase in employment
of almost 200 percent, and their employment force as a percent of total employment increased from 1.5 percent to 3.8 percent.

Total unemployment decreased modestly during the period from 1960-
1969. However, the percentage decrease in the number of nonminority unemployed workers was relatively greater than the decrease for Blacks. While the
average decrease for the entire labor force was 27 percent, the unemployment of
Spanish-speaking actually increased by more than a hundred percent. The unemployment of Blacks as a percent of total unemployment was 20.4 in 1960 and
over the nine-year span decreased fractionally to 20.1 percent, while unemployment for the Spanish-speaking rose from 2.4 percent to 6.7 percent.

Unemployment rates have remained highest for Blacks. In 1960 the unemployment rate for Blacks was 10.2 percent; by 1969 it had decreased to 6.4 per-
dent. However, this still left Blacks with an unemployment rate twice that of
nonminorities. The unemployment rate for the Spanish-speaking was 8.5 percent
in 1960 and dropped to 6 percent in 1969. The ratio of the Black unemployment rate to the Spanish-speaking unemployment rate increased from 1.7 in
1960 to 2 in 1969, indicating that the Spanish-speaking fared slightly better
than the Blacks over the 10-year period. In both cases, however, unemployment
rates remained above the nonminority national average.

In late 1968, when Black Capitalism made its debut, along with other
federal programs, it came at a time when the U.S. economy was slipping into the
1969-70 recession. As a consequence of the recession, the position gains from
Black Capitalism were nullified, and in 1972 the unemployment level of Blacks
had risen to 10.0 percent, from 6.4 percent in 1969. The Spanish-speaking
minority were also adversely affected. By 1972 their unemployment rates had
risen to 7.6 from 6 percent.

In investigating these two minority groups' income characteristics, we see
that from 1960 to 1969 the median family income (Table 5-2) of Blacks and

Table 5-1
Trends in Employment—Minorities and Nonminorities

	1960	1969	1972
Employment (thousands)	65,778	77,902	81,702
Black and Other Races	6,927	8,384	8,628
Spanish-Speaking	1,004	2,979	3,123
Nonminority	57,846	66,539	69,951
Percent of Total			
Black and Other Races	10.5	10.8	10.7
Spanish-Speaking	1.5	3.8	3.8
Unemployment (thousands)	3,852	2,831	4,840
Black and Other Races	787	570	956
Spanish-Speaking	93	190	255
Nonminorities	2,970	2,071	3,629
Percent of Total			
Black and Other Races	20.4	20.1	19.8
Spanish-Speaking	2.4	6.7	5.3
Unemployment rate (percent)			
Total	5.5	3.5	5.6
Black and Other Races	10.2	6.4	10.0
Spanish-Speaking	8.5	6.0	7.6
Nonminority	4.9	3.0	5.0
Ratio: Black/Nonminority	2.1	2.1	2.0
Black/Spanish-Speaking	1.2	1.1	1.3
Spanish-Speaking/			
Nonminority	1.7	2.0	1.5

Source: U.S. Department of Labor, Bureau of Labor Statistics, Andrew F. Brimmer, "Economic Developments in the Black Community," *Public Interest*, No. 34, Winter 1974, p. 147.

other minorities almost doubled, from approximately $3,233 to $6,191. During the same year, the median income of nonminority families increased from $5,835 to $9,794. As a result, the income gap between Blacks and other minorities and the nonminority community widened. The ratio of Black to nonminority median family income increased from 0.55 to 0.63.

Surprisingly, the 1969–70 recession did not have a pronounced income effect on Blacks who were employed. The ratio of Black to nonminority income decreased from 0.61 in 1969 to 0.60 in 1971, and further to 0.59 in 1972. However, in absolute terms, the income gap between Blacks and nonminority families increased from $3,795 to $4,685. These income figures are shown in Table 5-2.

The Spanish-speaking minority experienced a temporary decrease in the income gap in absolute terms after the 1969–70 recession. The proportion of Spanish-speaking to nonminority family income increased from 58 percent to 71 percent before decling to 66 percent in 1972.

In terms of both income and employment, the Spanish-speaking minority

Table 5-2
Trends in Income for Minorities and Nonminorities

	1960	1969	1971	1972
Median Family Income (current dollars)				
Total	5,620	9,433	10,825	11,116[a]
Black and Other Races[b]	3,233	6,191	n.a.	7,106
Black	n.a.	5,999	6,440	6,864
Spanish-Speaking	n.a.	5,641	7,548	7,595
Nonminority	5,835	9,794	10,672	11,549
Income Gap				
Nonminority/Black or Other Races	2,602	3,603	n.a.	4,443
Nonminorities/Black	n.a.	3,795	4,232	4,685
Spanish-Speaking/Black	n.a.	(358)	1,108	0.731
Spanish-Speaking/ Nonminority	n.a.	4,153	3,124	3,954
Ratio: Black and Other Races	0.55	0.63	n.a.	0.62
Black/Nonminority	n.a.	0.61	0.60	0.59
Spanish-Speaking/ Nonminority	n.a.	0.58	0.71	0.66
Spanish-Speaking/Black	n.a.	0.95	1.16	1.12

[a]Data for 1972 for Spanish-Speaking Minority are average of March 1972 and March 1973 figures.
[b]Approximately 90% of this category are Black.
Source: U.S. Department of Commerce, Bureau of the Census and Andrew F. Brimmer, "Economic Developments in the Black Community," *Public Interest*, No. 34, Winter 1974.

seems to have fared better than the Blacks. The extent of this relative well-being is not certain however. Among Spanish-speaking communities, the accuracy of data collecting is questionable and presents a major concern. In an interview with a community spokesman for the Spanish-speaking, a New York City man-power analyst observed:

> Before you recognize people's needs, you first have to recognize the people. This has not been done. Information on employment and un-employment, for example, is gathered for two groups (1) whites, and (2) negroes and other minority races. This puts us in the bag of being a race when we are an ethnic group. Some of us are brown, some are white, some black, and some red. We get violent about this kind of thing. It shows us the continued bind we're in and when it comes to getting accurate data and documentation on 16 million Spanish-speaking Americans.[16]

In fact, there are added discrepancies when the Spanish-speaking are lumped together. For example, within the Spanish-speaking minorities, Mexican-Americans and Puerto Ricans fared worse than the overall Spanish-speaking

Table 5-3
Ethnic Characteristics of Poverty Population in 1970[a]

Ethnic Origin	Percentage in Poverty
Total Population	12.6%
Nonminority	9.9
Spanish Origin	24.3
Mexican-Americans	28.0
Puerto Rican	29.2
Cuban	13.7
Other	14.0
Blacks	33.6

[a]Poverty threshold income was approximately $3,900.

Source: U.S. Department of Commerce, U.S. Bureau of the Census, *Current Population Reports*, Series P–20, No. 224, October, 1975.

median. In 1970 the median family income for all Spanish-speaking minorities was $7,334. However, the Mexican-American median family income was $7,117 in 1970, and the Puerto Rican was $5,975, which placed them at approximately $300 less than the median income for Blacks. Puerto Ricans were obviously well below the Spanish-speaking average.

According to a recent federal study, after incomes were adjusted to take into account such factors as family size, sex, and age of family head, number of children, and farm or nonfarm residence, 24.3 percent of the Spanish-speaking, or 2.2 million Spanish-speaking Americans were living in poverty. Of these, 82 percent were Mexican-Americans or Puerto Ricans. These results are shown in Table 5-3. For these two sub-groups, the percentages of persons living in poverty were 28 and 29.2, respectively. The comparable figure for all Americans was 12.6 percent, while for Blacks it was 33.6 percent. Clearly, the Spanish-speaking, and particularly Mexican-Americans and Puerto Ricans, are grouped together with Blacks at the bottom of the economic echelon.

The general level of poverty decreased over the period 1959–1968. In 1959 there were 38.7 million poor people in the United States. Of these, 9.9 million or 26 percent were Black, 28.3 or 73 percent were nonminority, and the rest were other minorities. By 1968, however, the total number of poor persons declined to 25.4 million, of which 7.6 million or 29.9 percent were Black, 17.4 million or 68.5 percent were nonminority, and 0.4 million were other minorities. Thus, though there was a general decrease in poverty, the proportion of Blacks who were able to escape poverty was less than that of nonminorities. The percent of Blacks in poverty increased by 3.9 percent, while that of nonminorities decreased by 4.5 percent. Furthermore, although poverty appears to be absolutely a greater problem for nonminorities, it is a relatively greater problem for minorities, since they comprise a greater proportion of the poor for their respective population size.

Federal Manpower Programs

As a result of the Economic Opportunity Act (EOA of 1964, federal manpower programs started placing greater emphasis on solving the job problem and developing occupational skills for the undereducated and unskilled members of minority groups.

Before discussing the level of participation among minorities in these manpower programs, it is probably worthwhile to list and discuss the various manpower programs.[17]

1. Manpower Development and Training Act (MDTA): offers institutional and on-the-job training (OJT) with the aim of developing general skills.
2. Job Opportunities in the Business Sector (JOBS): public and private efforts are combined to place hard-core disadvantaged in major corporations.
3. Neighborhood Youth Corps (NYC): develops job skills to provide earnings, increase work orientation, and improve school attendance of urban youth.
4. Job Corps: stresses occupational learning in nonresident training schools.
5. Work Incentive Program (WIN): helps the poor to become self-supporting and independent of public welfare; a special target within this program is families receiving aid to dependent children (AFDC).
6. Concentrated Employment Program (CEP): satisfies the needs of rural manpower.
7. Operation Mainstream: like CEP, except that it places greater emphasis on the older rural residents, providing them with work and income.
8. Public Employment Program (PEP): checks unemployment by creating temporary employment in public areas of need; the program was introduced following the 1969–70 recession.

The impact of these federal government manpower programs is difficult to determine; there are various factors to be considered in measuring their success. For instance, it is necessary to compare the experiences of enrollees in these programs with those of a similar group which did not participate in the programs, in order to assess objectively the effects of the programs. Personal work traits may also influence the results. Additionally, there is the problem of defining "success." Further, cost outlays in terms of tax expenditures versus earnings of employees from such programs are frequently impossible to measure. Even if measured, a program deemed unsuccessful now may produce more meaningful results in the long-run.

If existing manpower programs have failed to achieve a breadth in outreach among minorities, their insufficiency has been greatest among the Spanish-speaking population. The proportion of Spanish-speaking enrollees in manpower programs is lower than the proportion of any other disadvantaged group. For example, MDTA/OJT, which is responsible for developing the general occupational skills, has shown the poorest participation record for Spanish-speaking—approximately 10 percent, compared to 30 percent for nonminorities and 60 percent for Blacks. The National Alliance of Businessmen (NAB)/Job Opportunities for Better Skills, which involves the largest absolute number of Spanish-speaking, records their participation as only 13 percent, compared to 69 percent for Blacks and 24 percent for nonminorities.

Black participation in JOBS was approximately 50 percent, compared to 21 percent for Spanish-speaking persons, while corresponding figures in fiscal year 1972 for the concentrated employment program were 60 percent and 20 percent, respectively. Neighborhood Youth Corps (NYC) had probably the highest relative participation of Spanish-speaking persons.

Overall, the participation of Blacks and Spanish-speaking persons was greater than their relative proportion of the nation's population, but it has not been adequate to meet the skill needs of minorities. Furthermore, the major manpower programs in terms of dollars, number of trainees, and opportunities for upgrading skills have been the ones with the lowest rates of Spanish-speaking participation (MDTA, OJT, NAB/JOBS, and Job Corps). Programs with a relatively better participation ratio—NYC and Operation Mainstream, for example—have included few persons in other than work-support programs, where opportunities for long-term economic advancement are limited. Despite increases in Spanish-speaking enrollment in recent years, participation levels remain proportionally low.

Additionally, results of participation are poor in terms of completion of training, earnings, and job retention and upgrading. Monolinguals and other people with severe educational disadvantages are screened out. Programs are not tailored to meet language and cultural differences of their constituency.

Culture, Language and Mores

There is a strong sense of cultural uniqueness among the Spanish-speaking population.[18] This cultural awareness can be classified in four categories as it affects the success of manpower programs: (1) language, (2) cultural orientation, (3) ethnic isolation, and (4) other social and psychological factors.

To some extent, the sense of being socially different among Spanish-speaking Americans results from the high proportion of the group experiencing poverty, as well as from cultural and language differences. Comparative studies have shown that the use of Spanish is more prevalent among Mexican-Americans and Puerto Ricans who live in the U.S. than the use of English. The use of Spanish is facilitated by the availability of Spanish mass media and entertainment, and by the custom of using Spanish in the household. Consequently, many

Spanish-speaking persons find themselves communicating solely in Spanish. The language preference is further reinforced by community isolation and the tendency for the Spanish-speaking work force to gravitate toward the lesser skilled and lower paid occupations in which Spanish results in being the occupational argot.

According to the 1969 census figures, roughly 25 percent of the Spanish-speaking population were illiterate in English. For Puerto Ricans, the figure was 40.3 percent. In the case of Puerto Rican youths aged 10–24 years, about 20 percent were illiterate in English. Hence, manpower programs offered solely in English have limited success. These figures help to explain why the Spanish-speaking have had problems in horizontal and vertical socioeconomic mobility.

Some of the differences in mores among Spanish-speaking people are their outlook on material gains, sense of achievement, strong family ties, ethnic pride, *machismo,* and patriarchial structure. These attitudes affect their ability to conform to Anglo-Saxon employment settings. For example, the impersonal employer-employee relationship in the U.S. contradicts the informal intimate relation to which Spanish-speaking people are accustomed.

Recent studies indicate that as more members of the population permeate into the mainstream of American life, their interactions will lead to a greater absorption of the social mores of their Anglo peers. However, the roots of these values are deep-seated, and there is little basis for thinking that significant changes will take place in the near future.

For cultural and socioeconomic reasons, the Spanish-speaking population is predominantly landlocked in various enclaves throughout the wouthwestern United States. Consequently, an overwhelming majority live in self-contained barrios which are separated from the general community. This tendency strengthens the linguistic and cultural separation, which in turn limits occupational mobility and increases the transaction and psyche costs involved in participating in outside *barrio* manpower training programs.

Wealth Accumulation

Most research studying the economic development of minorities has stressed variables such as income and earnings. These variables have been studied because data on them has been more readily available in the past. However, income and earnings do not completely depict the economic status of minorities because they fail to account for the relative wealth position of minority households. This section discusses the wealth accumulation of Black families by income levels and compares it to wealth accumulation of nonminority families in similar income categories.[19]

The first comprehensive data on relative wealth accumulation position of the Black population was provided in 1967 by the Survey of Economic Opportunity. Table 5–4 presents data on wealth accumulation of Black and White

Table 5-4
Total Net Wealth of White and Black Families, by Income Class (Mean Amounts in Dollars)

Income Class	Net Wealth		Ratio of Black to White Wealth	Wealth-Income Ratio[a]	
	White	Black		White	Black
$ 0–2,499	$ 10,681	$ 2,148	20.1	7.51	1.61
2,500–4,999	13,932	2,239	16.1	3.75	0.62
5,000–7,499	13,954	4,240	30.4	2.25	0.69
7,500–9,999	16,441	6,021	36.6	1.91	0.70
10,000–14,999	24,304	8,694	35.8	2.04	0.74
15,000–19,999	43,413	20,533	47.3	2.58	1.22
20,000 and over	101,009	30,195	29.9	3.37	1.26
All units	20,153	3,779	18.8	2.58	0.81

[a]Evaluated at mean income within each income class.

Source: Henry Terrell, "Wealth Accumulations of Black and White Families," *Journal of Finance*, Vol. 26, No. 2 (May 1971), p. 364.

families, standardized by income level. It is evident from the data that as an aggregate group the net wealth of Black families was only 18.8 percent of the net wealth of White families, indicating that Black families possess less than one-fifth of the total wealth accumulation of nonminority families.

Table 5-4 examines Blacks' net wealth position as a percentage of Whites' net wealth for various income classes. It shows that for lower incomes, such as $2,500-4,999, the Black to White ratio was only 16.1 percent. But for higher income ranges, this ratio steadily increases to a high of 47.3 percent for the $15,000–$19,999 income range, before dropping sharply to 29.9 percent in the over $20,000 category. This drop can probably be explained largely by the fact that this category is open-ended and therefore includes a much larger number of the more affluent nonminority members of society. An interesting observation that can be made about the ratios is that the largest increase occurs from the $5,000–$7,499 class, while the corresponding population increase for Black families is over 89 percent.

Economically speaking, this suggests a very low income elasticity (dW/dI) (I/W) for Whites across these two income categories, compared to the income elasticity for Blacks. The elasticity coefficient for Whites is 0.003 as compared to 1.34 for Blacks.[20] The question that can be raised is: why is there a difference in income elasticities for these two income levels?

In general, evidence indicates that Black families at any observed income level have substantially less wealth than White families. This inequity for any given income class is explained by Terrell through his use of Friedman's theory of permanent income. For the sake of review, let us begin by discussing the permanent income hypothesis. The conditional statements are that:

$$y \quad = y_p + y_t$$

$$C \quad = C_p + C_t$$

$$C_p \quad = k(i, w, u) Y_p$$

$$r_{y_t y_p} = r_{y_t C_p} = r_{y_t C_t}$$

where r is the correlation coefficient.

In the model, two components are distinguished by their maturity—permanent and transitory income (y_p and y_t). Consumption (C) is composed of similar permanent and transitory components (C_p and C_t). Further, permanent consumption is viewed as directly proportional to permanent income or stated mathematically, $C_p \propto y_p$ or $C_p = ky_p$. However, the proportionality constant, k, is seen as a function of three other variables: i, the rate of interest; w, the ratio of physical wealth to income, and u, a proportionality variable determining the consumer units' tastes and preferences for wealth versus consumption. Further, u is in itself a function of the size and age distribution of the consumption unit, and

Table 5-5
Net Wealth Accumulation for White and Black Families

Type of Asset	Mean Accumulation Per Family (Absolute Amount)			Estimated Aggregate Holdings (billions of dollars)	
	White	Black	Ratio	White	Black
Nonfinancial Assets					
Equity in Home	$ 6,511	$2,125	32.6	$ 359.2	$12.7
Equity in Cars and Trucks	1,033	309	29.9	57.0	1.9
Equity in Other Real Estate	1,868	436	23.3	103.1	2.6
Farm Equity	2,769	309	11.2	152.8	1.9
Business Equity	1,904	216	11.3	105.1	1.3
Subtotal	$14,085	$3,395	24.1	$ 777.2	$20.4
Financial Assets					
Value of Stocks	2,631	39	1.5	145.2	0.2
Money in Banks	2,955	296	10.0	163.0	1.9
Government Bonds	482	49	10.2	26.6	0.3
Subtotal	$ 6,068	$ 384	6.3	$ 334.8	$ 2.3
Total, All Assets	$20,153	$3,779	18.8	$1,112.0	$22.7

Source: Henry Terrell, "Wealth Accumulations of Black and White Families," *Journal of Finance*, Vol. 26, No. 2 (May 1971), p. 367.

of the standard deviation of the probability distribution of the proportion of transitory components to their corresponding permanent components.[21]

In considering the determinants of consumption, Friedman argues that income data are inadequate for comparing the relative long-run income status for Black families because they fail to show the history of lower past incomes and the expected lower future incomes of Black families.[22]

Tables 5-5 and 5-6 examine the accumulation, distribution and aggregates of net wealth for both Black and White families. The figures show extreme amounts of structural difference in the wealth portfolio of Black and White families. The SEO data indicates that considering all assets, both financial and nonfinancial, Blacks had only 18.8 percent of the total assets alone. A Black family had a total of $384 in financial assets. This constituted only 10.2 percent of its total assets of $3,779 and only 6.3 percent of the White family's average financial assets; the White family had 30 percent of its total assets in stocks, bonds, and cash.

Black family nonfinancial assets accounted for 90 percent of their total assets compared to 70 percent for the White family, and the Black family's non-financial assets constituted 24.1 percent of the White family's nonfinancial

Table 5-6
Aggregate Distribution of Net Worth for White and Black Families

Type of Asset	Distribution of Holdings (percent)		Black Share of Total[a] (percent)
	White	Black	
Nonfinancial Assets			
Equity in Home	32.3%	56.2%	3.4%
Equity in Cars and Trucks	5.1	8.2	3.2
Equity in Other Real Estate	9.3	11.5	2.5
Farm Equity	13.7	8.2	1.2
Business Equity	9.4	5.7	1.2
Subtotal	69.9	89.8	2.6
Financial Assets			
Value of Stocks	13.1	1.0	0.13
Money in Banks	14.7	7.8	1.1
Government Bonds	2.4	1.3	1.1
Subtotal	30.1	10.2	0.7
Total, All Assets	100%	100%	2.0

[a]This is the Black share of the total for the entire Black and White population and does not include holdings of the less than 1 percent of the non-Black minority population.

Source: Henry Terrell, "Wealth Accumulations of Black and White Families," *Journal of Finance*, Vol. 26, No. 2 (May 1971), p. 367.

assets. Blacks had the greatest portion of their assets in housing (56.2 percent), compared to 32.3 percent for the White family.

Overall, it was estimated that Black families had approximately 0.7 percent of all the financial assets. Black families displayed a definite tendency toward accumulation of consumption-oriented assets, such as cars, trucks, and housing, while White families hold a greater share of their nonfinancial assets in income-producing assets, such as farms, real estate, and business equity. This difference in wealth preferences is not surprising, given the discretionary investment constraints imposed on minorities.

Black family units with their substantially lower levels of income are forced out of basic necessity to invest their incomes in the more common physical assets, such as cars and housing. Consequently, there are no compounded returns over time. The degree of exclusion experienced by Blacks can be observed by examining the stock/business equity ratio for White and Black families. This is 1.38 for Whites and 0.18 for the Black family, indicating the latter's lack of access and participation.

Aside from the comparative size and composition of Black wealth accumulation, it is important to examine the relative degree of concentration of wealth among Black and White families. One method is through the use of the Gini Index.[c]

The data in Table 5-7 indicate two related findings. First, the distribution of net wealth is more uneven than the distribution of income and this is true for Blacks, Whites, and all family units taken as a whole. Second, income among

---

[c]The Gini Index of concentration is defined as the proportion of the total area under the diagonal that is between the diagonal and the Lorenz curve. Mathematically, the Index GI can be expressed as follows:

$$GI = \frac{\alpha}{\alpha + \beta} = \frac{\text{Area between curve and diagonal}}{\text{Area under diagonal}}$$

$$= 1 - \frac{\alpha}{\alpha + \beta}$$

Since the cumulative percent on each axis adds to 100, the area under the diagonal equals ½. Therefore,

$$GI = 1 - \frac{\beta}{½} = 1 - 2(\text{area under curve})$$

Now, if the equation of the curve is known, the area under the curve can be calculated as follows:

$$\int_0^1 f(u)\,du$$

where $f(u)$ represents the equation of the Lorenz curve as a function of the percent of units. If not, we can still approximate the area under the curve by assuming that the curve is a straight line between any two points, for then the area of the trapezium over any segment of the curve can be calculated as follows:

$$(f_{i+1} - f_i)\left(\frac{Y_i + Y_{i+1}}{2}\right)$$

Table 5-7
Gini Coefficients of Wealth Distribution and Its Components among White and Black Families

Asset Type	All Families			Families Reporting Accumulation		
	White	Black	Total	White	Black	Total
Government Bonds	0.942	0.983	0.946	0.774	0.785	0.776
Money in Banks	0.792	0.914	0.815	0.739	0.730	0.744
Value of Stocks	0.963	0.994	0.966	0.783	0.566	0.784
Equity in Farm	0.991	0.992	0.993	0.621	0.632	0.629
Equity in Business	1.074	1.049	1.075	0.773	0.869	0.777
Equity in Home	0.682	0.850	0.700	0.436	0.483	0.441
Equity in Other Real Estate	1.060	0.978	1.061	0.744	0.641	0.743
Equity in Cars and Trucks	0.658	0.903	0.681	0.553	0.650	0.561
Net Wealth	0.694	0.823	0.715	0.671	0.712	0.680
Family Income (SEO)	0.383	0.416	0.392	0.380	0.412[a]	0.389
Family Income (Census, 1966)	0.343	0.385	0.352	—	—	—

[a]Refers to all non-Whites.
Source: Henry Terrell, "Wealth Accumulation of Black and White Families: The Empirical Evidence," op. cit., p. 269.

where f_i and y_i refer to the abscissa and ordinate in the Lorenz curve. Summing the area of similar trapeziums, the area under the curve is

$$\sum_{i=1}^{k} (f_{i+1} - f_i) \left(\frac{Y_i + Y_{i+1}}{2}\right)$$

Then the Gini coefficient GI can be expressed as

$$GI = 1 - 2 \sum_{i=1}^{k} (f_{i+1} - f_i) \left(\frac{Y_i + Y_{i+1}}{2}\right)$$

$$GI = 1 - \sum_{i=1}^{k} (f_{i+1} - f_i) (Y_i + Y_{i+1})$$

or using integrals, if $f(u)$ is known,

$$= 1 - 2 \int_{0}^{1} f(u) du)$$

It should be noted that theoretically, if the area under the curve is zero, the Gini coefficient equals 1, implying total inequality, and if the area under the curve is 1/2, the Gini coefficient equals 0. In reality, however, while considering all families, the requirement that the vertical axis aggregate be summed from zero to 100 percent may be violated since some families may own a negative share of wealth. This gives negative values for certain measures of areas, which when summed up may give a net negative area and consequently a Gini coefficient greater than one.

Black families is less evenly distributed than among White families. (This is particularly true for SEO data as compared to the Census data.)

Examining net wealth Gini coefficients, the index for Black families was 0.823 compared to 0.694 for White families, indicating that Black families had a more uneven distribution of wealth, thus reinforcing the statement that economic purchasing power as a whole is less evenly distributed among Blacks than among nonminorities.

The right-hand side of Table 5-7 presents the coefficients recomputed for those units reporting positive accumulation in specific asset types. This was done to account for the fact that the lack of diffusion of asset ownership in some areas made the overall Gini parameters difficult to interpret.[23] The recomputed coefficients show no significant change for income distribution, but a substantial reduction in the values for wealth accumulation for White, Black, and the total number of families. In comparative terms, the drop in these values was greatest for the Blacks, but there still remained a more pronounced uneven distribution of net wealth among Blacks than among Whites. This difference may be due to lack of accountability and reporting of wealth accumulation by Black families.

The general findings on wealth accumulation demonstrate the pervasive effect of the past on the current economic status of the Black minority population. In cases of relative size, composition, and concentration, wealth accumulation, a Black household has less net wealth than its White counterpart. This evidence suggests that economic parity for Black families and other minorities in general will not be achieved when the current annual income gap between minorities and nonminorities is eliminated because a considerable wealth gap will still remain intact as a past reminder of earlier economic deprivation. The current status of minorities is a result of past practices of the ruling class. And it is important not to lose sight of the fact that current data on wealth and income reflect discrimination over time. Therefore, the effect of such variables on observed outcomes is misleading and should be analyzed with caution. As it was succinctly stated by a colleague:

> It should be clear to all that the current status of blacks is in large measure attributable to limitations placed on them in the past. In this sense, no econometric study which makes use of variables whose present values are dependent on past discrimination can separate out the effect of these variables and the process which gave rise to them. That is to say, current data on the distribution of income, occupation and education reflect discrimination over time. Therefore, the effect of such variables on observed outcomes is misleading. The coefficients do not mean the same thing for blacks as they do for whites. Discrimination affects both the distribution of the income, occupation, education variables and their effect on observed outcomes.
>
> The likelihood that a black person will complete a given number of years of schooling is less than it is for a white person. In addition, the

quality of the schooling is likely to be poorer for the black person. If education is a key variable in determining occupation and income, then the black person will also have a lower occupation and less income. Discrimination affects the observed outcomes in yet another way. Blacks with the same education, as measured by school years and achievement do not receive as high returns on their investment in education as whites. It has been argued that differences in employment security of blacks and whites is partially due to differences in their distribution of job skills and partially to discrimination. However, since the distribution of job skills is itself a function of discrimination, this argument understates the effect of discrimination on the economic status of blacks.[24]

Socioeconomic Profile of the
Mexican-American

The total Spanish-surname population at present is estimated at about 11 million. Almost 60 percent of this population resides in the five southwestern states of California, New Mexico, Arizona, Texas, and Colorado. Within these five southwestern states, East Los Angeles, situated in Southern California, comprises the largest single concentration of Mexican-Americans, often synonymously referred to as "Chicanos." This section discusses the economic characteristics of the Mexican-American community in East Los Angeles (ELA) in terms of employment, income, education, and housing. At times, comparisons have been made with other surrounding nonminority communities wherever appropriate.

The estimated population of the East Los Angeles area, as of the 1970 census, was 260,238. The ethnic composition, as of 1970, was 78.5 percent Mexican-American, 1.9 percent Black, 3.9 percent Oriental, 15.9 percent Anglos and others. The Mexican-American population for Los Angeles County amounted to 15 percent in 1970, indicating that the ELA area had five times the number of Chicanos as did Los Angeles County, in general.

The age distribution of the populace according to the 1970 Census was as follows: 33–37 percent were 14 years and under; 10.0 percent were 15 to 19 years of age; 8.2 percent were 20 to 24 years of age; 23.6 percent were 25 to 44 years of age; 16.1 percent were 45 to 64 years of age; and 8.3 percent were 65 years and over. This data indicates that approximately 58 percent were able to participate in the labor force. The median age for the ELA area was 22.4 years for males and 24.7 years for females, compared to 28.2 and 30.4 in Los Angeles County for nonminority males and females, respectively, indicating that the area as a whole has a relatively young population.

Housing. Housing in East Los Angeles can be classified as poor, with many of the structures in a run-down dilapidated condition. The problem has been aggravated by "red lining" practices which have disabled the residents of the area in obtaining conventional financing to improve their homes or to construct new dwellings.

In 1970 there were 74,399 housing units in East Los Angeles of which 26,519 or 35.64 percent were owner occupied; 46,238 or 62.15 percent were non-owner occupied; and 1,642 or 2.21 percent were vacant. This distribution indicates that there were almost twice as many people renting homes as there were owning their own homes. In the long run, the combination of low income, unemployment, and red lining practices by financial institutions will continue to prevent Chicanos in ELA from changing their wealth position.

Of the 74,399 housing units, about 56,000 or 74 percent of the units were built prior to 1940, which indicates the poor housing in the area. Only about 4 to 5 percent of the structures as of 1970 were built after 1968.

If the present housing trend continues, it has serious ramifications for the residents of East Los Angeles. Since 2.2 percent of the houses are vacant, and few new housing units are being developed, any substantial increase in population will result in over-crowded or unhoused community members.

A study of the Mexican-American people indicated that in Southwestern metropolitan areas, Chicanos had a 34.6 percent incidence of overcrowded housing, compared to 21.8 percent for non-Whites and only 7.7 percent for non-minorities.

Another added obstacle is that private investors are unwilling to commit funds for building new dwellings because of their concern for short pay-back periods. Low income also adds to these people's inability to obtain conventional mortgage financing.

A parallel situation is evident in the refurbishing of existing structures. Since 62 percent of the buildings are under absentee ownership, the landlords avoid investing in the existing units for fear that their investment will not generate rental receipts sufficient to cover the increases in property taxes and the cost of the improvement loans.

The housing problem of East Los Angeles cannot be treated in isolation since dilapidated housing commands low rents, which in turn attract an excess supply of low-skilled workers who command low wages. Also, there is an influx of illegal aliens from across the border who are seeking cheap housing. The result is a community with a surplus of low-skilled workers whose future potential of increasing its income to a parity level is nullified. Thus, the poor housing problem in effect reinforces itself indirectly.

Education. Presently ELA is served by two public school districts and five Catholic elementary schools. The only college located in East Los Angeles is a community college which serves both ELA and surrounding communities.

Language problems and cultural differences have created special needs for Mexican-American students in ELA that have not been met. Educationally,

Mexican-Americans have experienced a drop-out rate near 50 percent.[d] However, the Census Bureau reported recently a rise in education for young Spanish-speaking men and women. A nationwide survey in March 1974 showed that 56 percent of Spanish-speaking men and women in the 20-to-24 age group had completed four years of high school or more, compared with only 37 percent of those 25 years old and over. The report said that in 1974 of the Spanish origin population 25 to 34 years old, 45 percent were high school graduates; by March 1974, this proportion had increased to 51 percent. Placing these figures in context, the report noted that about 20 percent of the Spanish origin population 25 years old and over had less than five years of school. For the whole U.S. population, this figure is five percent for men and four percent for women.[25]

If one views education as a consumption or investment good, then it is obvious that the consumer or investor in East Los Angeles, despite the educational gains noted above, frequently rejects the rendered service or the social returns which this type of education would offer. A large part of the rejection is due to lack of adequate bilingual education programs and the inability of the Mexican-American in ELA to see any future economic gains from remaining in school. For most see the future as offering only unskilled occupational opportunities which can be acquired with or without a secondary education. A recent study by the Los Angeles City School District in 1972 showed that a significant number of students speak only Spanish and limited English at grades 7 and 8. This language deficiency, coupled with the lack of suitable household accommodations encourages the exit of the majority of these students from the public school system.

Employment. In 1970, over 90 percent of the total East Los Angeles population was employed as private wage and salary workers. In 1970, manufacturing industries employed 40.4 percent of the labor force, while retail trades and services employed 20.6 percent and 21.3 percent of the total labor force, respectively.

Table 5-8 summarizes the percentage unemployment for East Los Angeles, the County of Los Angeles and the nation. The figures in Table 5-8 indicate that for any given year, except 1975, for which data was not available, the unemployment rate in ELA was at least 32 percent greater than in the County of Los Angeles, and 59 percent greater than in the nation as a whole. The unemployment picture is further examined in Table 5-9 which presents unemployment within East Los Angeles in accordance to specific ethnic groups and age. Data therein shows that the Chicano minority and Blacks in ELA had higher unemployment rates for all ages than nonminorities. While the unemployment for

---

[d]For an explanation of why there is an early withdrawal from the American educational system by Mexican-Americans, see J.R. Dominguez, "Issues of Equity and Efficiency in the Public Educational Financing of the State of California," National Urban Coalition Monograph, July, 1974.

Table 5–8
Unemployment Rates for East Los Angeles County and U.S. for
Selected Years

	1960	1965	1970	1975
East Los Angeles	13.0	7.1	7.8	n.a.
Los Angeles County	5.7	4.5	5.9	10.0
United States	5.5	4.5	4.9	8.9

Source: U.S. Department of Commerce, Bureau of the Census, 1960, 1965, 1970
and Labor Force Characteristics, 1975.

Table 5–9
Unemployment Levels in East Los Angeles for Chicano, Blacks,
and Nonminority, by Age and Sex, 1973

	Chicano	Black	Nonminority
Total, 16 years and older	7.5	9.3	4.3
Males, 20 years and older	5.3	5.9	2.9
Females, 20 years and older	7.2	8.5	4.3
Both sexes, 16–19 years	19.8	31.4	12.4

Source: McKay, Roberta V., "Employment and Unemployment Among Americans of Spanish Origin," Monthly Labor Review, April 1974, pp. 12–16.

males 20 years and over was lowest at 5.3 percent, the 16–19 age group had a
total unemployment rate of 19.8 percent. The corresponding rates for Blacks
was 31.4 percent, while nonminorities had a rate of only 12.6 percent, indicating
a higher level of unemployment for minority youth.

There are several reasons for this high unemployment rate in East Los
Angeles. First of all, the median educational attainment in ELA is only 7.7, as
compared to 12.4 for Los Angeles County. This means that Mexican-Americans
are limited both in terms of occupational mobility and higher educational
advancement.[26]

Secondly, most of the ELA work force either brings to the community
previous agricultural skills or limited nontransferable skills from the service or
manufacturing industries, resulting in a lack of skill diversification. In 1966, only
20 percent of all Mexican-American workers in California worked in white-collar
jobs, comprised mostly of clerical and sales positions.[27] Consequently, the work
force in East Los Angeles lacks the endowed potentials to move into new occupational areas of production, particularly those types of occupations which
yield monopolistic rents. This problem is both an outgrowth of and compounded
by employment discrimination.

Income Distribution.   In 1970, 62.3 percent of the families in East Los
Angeles earned between $6,000 and $24,000, compared to 72.3 percent for Los

Angeles County. In Table 5-10 we see the dollar distribution of incomes in East Los Angeles. The corresponding percentage distribution of incomes is shown in Figure 5-2. Examining incomes for the selected years 1960, 1965 and 1970, we see that in 1965, 62.2 percent of the families received less than $6,000 annual income. By 1970, the percentage of families in the less than $6,000 income bracket had decreased to 36.5 percent.

The general rise in family income was also noticed for families earning $25,000; however, still less than 2 percent of the population were enjoying this income level. While most income categories showed an increase from 1965 to 1970, the lower income groups below $8,000 experienced a decrease. The largest increase within any one category, however, was experienced by the $15,000 to $25,000 and over category. Over the 5 years from 1965 to 1970, the percent of families in this group increased from 1.95 to 10.0, about a five-fold increase.

The figures for family income in Figure 5-2 are somewhat misleading if we fail to consider the number of persons per household. The figure for East Los Angeles is 3.45, compared to 2.89 for Los Angeles County. This means that the relative income per person is less in East Los Angeles than in the County as a whole. Furthermore, in 1970, 16.7 percent of the families in ELA were below poverty level, and 31.2 percent were on public assistance.

Receipts and Representation

As of 1969 there were approximately one hundred thousand firms owned by members of the Spanish-speaking minority; their receipts were $3.3 billion. According to a recent report released by the Department of Commerce's Bureau of the Census, gross receipts of firms owned by persons of Spanish-speaking origin increased by an estimated $5.3 billion in 1972. This represented an over-

Table 5-10
Distribution of Family Income for East Los Angeles by Income Category, for Selected Years

Income Levels	1960	1965	1970
$ 0–$5999	21,403	31,370	21,298
6000–$7999	11,739	8,876	10,209
10,000–$14,999	5,098	4,098	12,244
15,000–$24,999	589	982	5,146
25,000 & over	123	131	675
All Families	45,188	50,435	58,319

Source: Garcia, Secundino M., et al., "Manpower Assessment of East Los Angeles," Unpublished Field Study Project, Graduate School of Management, University of California, Los Angeles, May 1974.

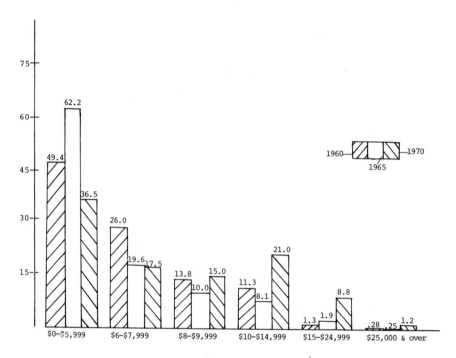

Figure 5–2. Percentage Family Income Distribution for East Los Angeles by Income Category for Selected Years. Source: U.S. Department of Commerce, Bureau of the Census.

all increase of $1.9 billion from the previous survey in 1969, which translates into a 18 percent annum increase in revenue. In 1972, the number of firms owned by the Spanish-speaking amounted to 120,108, which represented a twenty percent increase from the year 1969. About one-fourth or 28,166 of these firms are located in California and they account for one-fourth of the aggregate revenues, $1.3 billion. Texas ranks second with 23,651 Spanish-speaking owned firms, and their gross volume amounts to one billion dollars annually. The update report, a follow-up of the earlier publication, *Minority-Owned Business: 1969*, showed that over the three-year period, the concentration of Spanish-owned firms in certain types of industries had not changed. The Spanish-speaking still were highly concentrated in retail trade and selected service, two of the industries which have proven to be the least profitable. One encouraging note is that the largest percentage increases in volume were experienced in the least represented areas of manufacturing (126 percent) and the construction industry (125 percent).

The largest increase in the number of firms and amount of receipts took place in construction and in retail trade. Construction companies increased in number by 6,656, and retail outlets increased by 8,932. Their gross total receipts were augmented by $731 million and $375 million, respectively.

Owners of these firms included Mexican-Americans, Puerto Ricans, Cubans, and others of Spanish American ancestry. For the same year there was an approximate total of 322,000 minority-owned business enterprises, with total receipts of $10.6 billion. One-half of these, 163,000, were Black-owned with total receipts of $4.5 billion. Other minorities, including American Indians and Orientals, owned 59,000 firms with receipts of $2.8 billion. These participation values are presented in Tables 5-11 and 5-12.

Within the minority business community, Blacks had the highest representation, owning 50.62 percent of all the minority-owned firms and the Spanish-speaking and other minorities accounted for the remaining half. The Black-owned firms generated 42.5 percent of the total receipts of $10.6 billion, while Spanish-speaking and other minorities accounted for 31.13 percent and 26.41 percent of the receipts, respectively. However, the revenue share of other minorities and the Spanish-speaking was greater than that of Blacks, as can be seen in Table 5-12. Other minorities averaged about $47,457 per firm. The per capita figure for the Spanish-speaking was $33,000 per firm. This pattern of receipts can be explained by the larger number of small-scale single proprietorships among Blacks, which diluted the revenue base, giving rise to smaller revenue shares. Blacks with the highest number of firms had the lowest receipts per firm, while other minorities with the smallest number had the greatest volume of receipts per capita.

While these figures for the number of minority-owned firms and their gross receipts may on first impression seem impressive, a more accurate picture can be discerned by examining their level of participation, as shown in Table 5-12,

Table 5-11
Structure of Minority Business Community

Business Communities	Total Number of Firms	Percentage of Total in United States	Percentage of Total Minority Business Community
Total:			
United States	7,489,000	100.00%	—
Minority	321,958	4.00	100.00%
Black	163,000	2.00	50.62
Spanish-Speaking	100,000	1.00	31.06
Other Minorities	59,000	0.78	18.32

Source: *Minority-Owned Businesses: 1969*, U.S. Department of Commerce, Bureau of the Census, MB-1, August 1971.

Table 5-12
Receipt Distribution of Minority Firms

Business Communities	Total Receipts (billions $)	Percentage of Total United States	Percentage of Total Minority Business Community	Per Capita Receipts
Total United States	$1,498.	100.00%	—	$200,027.00
Minority	10.6	0.70	100.00%	32,919.00
Black	4.5	0.30	42.45	27,607.00
Spanish-Speaking	3.3	0.22	31.13	33,000.00
Other Minorities	2.8	0.18	26.41	47,457.00

Source: *Minority-Owned Businesses: 1969*, op. cit.

which shows that as of 1969 there were 7,489,000 firms in the United States whose total receipts amounted to $1,498 billion. The consolidated representation of all racial and ethnic minority firms amounted to less than 5 percent. This commercial disparity is further evidenced by their disproportional share of total business receipts, which amounted to only seven-tenths of one percent of the $1,498 billion gross figure. This fractional representation reflects the general climate of acceptance that American business has shown towards minority enterprise.

Finance, Insurance, and Real Estate Industries. Of the total number of firms in the United States, 16 percent could be classified as members of either the finance, insurance, or real estate industries. The firms in these three industries generated a business volume of $86.67 billion, and accounted for 5.8 percent of the total receipts of all companies in the United States.[e] The number of minority firms from these three industries constituted 1.8 percent, and their total revenues of $539 million accounted for less than six-tenths of one percent of the combined receipts for these three industries.

The total receipts of $539 million by the 21,806 minority-owned firms represented 5 percent of the revenue generated by all minority firms. The finance, insurance, and real estate industries, when compared to other industries,

---

[e]Measurements of employment and receipts of minority-owned enterprises are examined for the following categories of business firms in the finance, insurance, and real estate industry: banking, credit agencies (other than banking), security services, commodity brokers, insurance carriers, insurance agents, such as brokers and services, real estate, holding companies, and other investment firms. The reason for surveying this group is that they have a direct or indirect influence on capital formation. Throughout the remaining section, the data presented either in discussion, tables or figures were derived and constructed from the statistics presented in the publication, *Minority-Owned Businesses: 1969*, op. cit. Whenever the data permits, the discussion will focus on the Mexican-American instead of the more general term of the Spanish-speaking.

Table 5-13

Distribution of Number and Receipts of All Minority-Owned Firms in the Finance, Insurance, and Real Estate Industries for Selected States

| Area | All Minority Firms | Finance, Insurance and Real Estate Firms | | Receipts of Finance, Insurance and Real Estate Firms (in thousands of dollars) | |
		Number	As Percent of All[a] Minority Firms	Gross	Average
United States	321,958	21,806	6.77%	$439,298	$24,731
California	64,165	6,100	9.51	85,518	14,019
Texas	37,284	1,650	4.43	20,901	12,667
Colorado	3,403	193	5.67	7,937	41,124

[a]Percentage figures are for each respective state and represent the proportion of minority-owned firms participating in finance, insurance, and real estate, as compared to the total number of minority firms participating in all industries.

provide a minor source of revenue for minorities. They are small *vis à vis* the total industry, as well as within the minority grouping.

Blacks owned 7,612 or approximately 35 percent of the firms in these industries, and their total annual volume of business was $228 million. The Spanish-speaking owned the largest number of firms among the minorities (7,865). However, they were concentrated in SIC categories which generated a smaller volume of revenue. Receipts per firm were $13,859 as compared to $37,835 for the Black enterprises. Other minorities showed less breadth in ownership. The number of firms for this group totaled 6,329.

Fifteen percent of all minority firms within these three industries were listed as employee-type firms.[f] The remaining 85 percent of the minority firms were single proprietorships with unpaid employees, which disproportionately accounted for only 16 percent of the gross receipts of all the minority-owned firms, showing results similar to those cited in chapter 2. Besides income differences existing between minority and nonminority firms, there is an obvious revenue disparity between those firms with employees and those without. It is apparent that some minority enterprises find it difficult to compete both inside and outside of the inner city.

Table 5-13 presents comparative data of the finance, insurance, and real estate industries for the United States, and for California, Texas, and Colorado. These states collectively represented 54 percent of the total number of minority firms involved in these three industries throughout the United States.

Data in Table 5-13 indicates that California houses 20 percent of all the minority firms in the United States for all industries. Texas accounts for approximately 12 percent of all minority enterprises, and Colorado, although housing a

---

[f]The Bureau's definition of an employee-type firm is a company which has one or more paid employees.

sizeable minority population, has a minimal representation of less than one percent. Besides accounting for the largest number of minority firms in all industries among these three states, California also had a greater percentage of firms in finance, insurance, and real estate. It accounted for roughly 30 percent of the 21,806 firms in these industries for the United States. Texas hosted 7½ percent of all firms involved in the three related industries, and Colorado's representation was eight-tenths of one percent. Clearly, California is the state that dominates in number. However, within Colorado, the 193 firms in these three industries account for 5.67 percent of all the minority firms within the State. This proportion was lower in Texas with 4.43 percent, but higher in California, with 9.51 percent of interstate representation for the finance, insurance, and real estate industries.

Gross receipts in California were $85.5 million, which were about four times as great as the receipts for Texas of $20.9 million, and eleven times the size of Colorado's $7.9 million. However, these figures are not an accurate comparative measure, since the total number of firms generating these figures is not the same in each state. An examination of average receipts per firm, then, indicates a different picture altogether. Colorado had highest receipts per firm, while the receipts of California and Texas were far below this average. This can be partially explained by the fact that these industries are much more developed and advanced, and the relative competition within California is much greater than in Texas and Colorado. For example, in California approximately one out of four firms participates in these industries, as opposed to one out of twelve in Texas and much fewer in Colorado. As a result, minority firms in these three industries are likely to be subjected to greater competitive pressures and to receive a smaller share of the market. It is axiomatic that any increase in the number of independent competitors inevitably leads to an increase in competition itself.

While the discussion so far has focused on all minority firms in those three industries, Tables 5-14 and 5-15 examine in particular the participation and revenue performance of Mexican-American firms in California, Texas, and Colorado. In all three states, Mexican-Americans, the predominant ethnic subset of the Spanish-speaking, accounted for over 90 percent of all Spanish-speaking owned proprietorships. Mexican-Americans represented approximately 50 percent of all minority firms in finance, insurance and real estate industries.[g]

California accounted for the largest number of Mexican-American firms and gross receipts, but per capita receipts for Mexican-American firms were considerably lower—$11,600 compared to $19,700 for Colorado, which had the highest per capita receipts. Here again the inverse relationship between number of firms and per capita receipts is again witnessed. Whereas the average receipts per firm for all minority firms in Colorado were $41,124, the corresponding figure for

---

[g]Wherever possible the discussion will attempt to focus on the business characteristics which pertain to Mexican-Americans. At times, this may not be consistently observed because of Bureau of the Census' limited inter-ethnic information disclosure, which is aimed at protecting the identity of the sample firms.

Table 5-14

Distribution of Number and Receipts of Mexican-American Firms in the Finance, Insurance, and Real Estate Industries for Selected States

Area	All Minority (AM) Firms	Spanish-Speaking (SS) Firms	Mexican-American Firms	Mexican-American Firms as a Percent of		Receipts of Mexican American Firms (in thousands of dollars)	
				AM Firms	SS Firms	Gross	Average Per Firm
California	6,100	2,558	2,442	42	96	$24,418.0	$11.6
Texas	1,650	955	930	58	97	11,112.0	11.9
Colorado	193	94	90	49	96	1,775.0	19.7

Mexican-American firms was only $19,700. Similar, but less drastic increases in per capita receipts are also noticed in the cases of Texas and California. This means that Mexican-Americans have experienced a small share of the receipts in geographical areas in which they are the predominant ethnic minority.

As was similarly true for all minorities, employee-type concerns constituted a smaller percentage of all the Mexican-American firms in these three related industries. In California, only 11.7 percent of all Mexican-American firms operated with one or more paid employees, while Texas and Colorado enjoyed percentile margins of 17.4 and 14.0, respectively. The striking feature is that in all cases employee firms' revenue performance is far superior to nonemployee firms. Mexican-American employee firms had average receipts per firm of $69,000 in California, $40,000 in Texas, and $114,000 in Colorado, indicating a consistently better revenue performance by employee-type firms.

Table 5-15

Distribution of Number and Receipts of Mexican-American Employee-Type Firms in the Finance, Insurance, and Real Estate Industries for Selected States

Area	Number of Firms	Employee-Type Firms		Receipts (in Thousands of Dollars)		Employees	
		Number	As Percent of Total	Gross	Average per Firms	Total	Per Firm
California	2,442	285	11.7	$19,737.0	$ 69.0	595	2
Texas	930	162	17.4[a]	7,738.0	48.0	334	2
Colorado	90	13	14.0	1,485.0	114.0	39	3
Total for States	3,462	460	13.3	28,960.0	83.6	968	4

[a]Figures for number of employees and gross receipts of Mexican-American employee-type firms in Texas were estimated, due to lack of breakdown in available data.

This can probably be explained by two factors. Firstly, the transactions within these industries require more than a single proprietor to manage all the related activities dictated by the natures of the business within these labor-intensive industries. Due to undercapitalization, many Mexican-American firms are unable to start with a paid staff and as a result of this smallness, they continue to operate with limited help, even though positive incremental revenues may be realized by increasing their work force. Consequently, those that are able to have paid employees manage to enjoy greater per capita revenues. Secondly, as explained earlier, Mexican-Americans in Colorado probably experience less severe competition than in California or Texas, and thus the few businessmen who do exist are able to gross a larger volume of receipts than in the other states.

Interethnic Distribution and Structure

Black real estate firms accounted for 72.57 percent of the total number of Black firms in the three related industries. Most of the Black companies operating within the category of finance related industries are involved principally in the used asset turnover of inner city dwellings. Their business activities do not for the most part involve new housing but rather second-hand transactions of existing structures. The figure for Blacks was moderately greater than the all-minority average of 60.26 percent or the Spanish-speaking average of 49.59 percent. The "catch-all" industry accounted for 26.7 percent of all the Spanish-speaking firms in the finance, insurance, and real estate industries, compared to the all-minority average of 9.63 percent and the Black average of 1.56 percent. This indicates that one-fourth of the Spanish-speaking firms surveyed could not be accurately identified.

The distribution of gross receipts showed greater skewness than the distribution of the number of firms. The largest diaparity of gross receipts was most apparent for insurance carriers. Black insurance carriers accounted for 46.4 percent of the gross receipts generated by the three related industries. Compared to this figure, the proportion of receipts of insurance carrier firms owned by all minorities was 21.24 percent, while for the Spanish-speaking it was less than 1 percent. This modest representation by the Spanish-speaking in the insurance industry was not reflected in real estate. Real estate receipts for Mexican-Americans accounted for 59.45 of the total receipts, compared to 35 percent for all minorities, and 27 percent for Blacks. Another area of minor participation was the field of banking. Blacks received a greater proportion of their receipts from banks (8.5 percent) as compared to the Spanish-speaking margin of 1.24 percent, but in either case both depended very little on banking as a source of revenue.

While the above discussion shows that Blacks and Spanish-speaking minorities had different major revenue sources, their average receipts per firm were

Table 5–16
Structure and Distribution of Black-Owned Firms, within the Finance, Insurance, and Real Estate Industries

Subindustry Classification	Gross Receipts (thousands of dollars)	Percent of Gross Receipts	Average Receipts per Firm (in dollars)	Number of Firms	Percent of all Firms
Insurance Carriers	$133,314	46.4%	$1,281,865	104	1.0%
Real Estate	77,916	27.1	14,105	5,524	73.0
Banking	24,445	8.5	698,428	35	0.5
Insurance Agents, Brokers, and Services	21,839	7.6	16,607	1,315	17.3
Credit Agencies Other than Banks	12,644	4.4	113,909	111	1.5
Securities, Commodity Brokers, and Services	6,765	2.4	26,322	257	3.4
Holding and Other Investment Companies	5,454	1.6	45,823	119	1.6
Combined Real Estate, Insurance, etc.	5,095	1.9	34,659	147	1.9
Finance, Insurance, and Real Estate Totals	$287,471	100%	$2,231,718	7,612	100%

Standard Deviation $\delta = 121,858$ Standard Deviation $\delta = 1,235,254$

Geometric Mean $\mu = 18,407$ Geometric Mean $\mu = 74,976$

significantly different in *only* the banking and insurance industries. In all three industry categories, Blacks and Spanish-speaking firms average receipts closely paralleled the mean values for all-minority-owned firms. Black insurance carriers had average receipts per firm of $1.3 million, as compared to $12,000 for Spanish-speaking insurance carriers. Also, Black banks had average receipts of $698,428 per bank, compared to $69,222 for the Spanish-speaking.

Insurance companies were the major source of income for the Black community, with gross receipts of $133 million, which accounted for roughly 46 percent of the total receipts of Black firms. The only other subindustry categories with sizable receipts were real estate and banking. Receipts of real estate firms owned by Blacks amounted to $77,916,000, and accounted for 27.1 percent of total receipts. These values are shown in Table 5-16. The number of insurance carriers amounted to only 104 or 1 percent of the total number of Black firms in the three related industries, although they generated high per firm receipts of $1.3 million. The small number of firms can probably be attributed to entry socio-economic barriers. The same statement can probably be said for Black banks, which had relatively high per firm receipts of $698,428.

The real estate industry, which requires small initial capital outlays, is relatively easier for an individual to enter and exit. This explains why, in the face of low per firm receipts, Black real estate firms accounted for almost 75 percent of the firms. By concentrating their activites in the real estate industry Blacks make themselves more vulnerable to economic misfortunes. First, the housing and real estate industry is a highly cyclical industry, with frequent up-swings and downswings. This means that Black firms would be gravitating towards an industry with greater instability and risk. Secondly, real estate is an occupational area which requires very little training, and mostly depends on the qualities of salesmanship that cannot be transferred to higher paying industries. As a result, most Black entrepreneurs are in effect prevented from entering into other industries which would develop for them a broader range of managerial skills.

In examining Mexican-American participation characteristics, we see that while the distribution of Black firms and their receipts was clearly discernible from the data in Table 5–16, the same was not true for Mexican-Americans. The picture is obscured by a large proportion of the firms (31.7 percent) and their receipts (26.0 percent) coming under the "catch-all" category. This industry

Table 5–17
Structure and Distribution of Mexican-American Owned Firms within the Finance, Insurance, and Real Estate Industries

Subindustry Classification	Gross Receipts (thousands of dollars)	Percent of Gross Receipts	Average Receipts per Firm (in dollars)	Number of Firms	Percent of all Firms
Real Estate	$32,696	51.0%	$ 11,656	2,805	46.8%
Finance, Insurance, and Real Estate Not Allocated by Industry	16,400	26.0	8,631	1,900	31.7
Insurance Agents, Brokers, and Services	7,579	12.0	11,414	664	11.0
Securities, Commodity Brokers, and Services	2,497	4.0	7,543	331	5.5
Credit Agencies Other than Banks	2,171	3.0	26,475	82	1.4
Holding and Other Investment Companies	1,091	2.0	7,905	138	2.3
Combined Real Estate, Investment, etc.	926	1.0	20,130	46	0.7
Banking	470	0.7	42,727	11	0.1
Insurance Carriers	126	0.2	11,454	11	0.1
Finance, Insurance, and Real Estate, Totals	$63,956	100%	$147,935	5,988	100%
	Standard Deviation $\delta = 30,889$		Standard Deviation $\delta = 33,035$		
	Geometric Mean $\mu = 2,221$		Geometric Mean $\mu = 13,773$		

division is shown in the information presented in Table 5-17. Table 5-17 also shows that banking and insurance, which accounted for 35 percent of total receipts for the Black firms, in contrast, generated only nine-tenths of one percent of the revenues for Mexican-Americans. This vast disparity in the participation by Mexican-Americans in the larger income generating industries is also seen when comparing aggregate gross receipts of Black banks and insurance companies, which had total gross receipts of $157 million, compared to roughly $600,000 for Mexican-American firms in the same industries.

The real estate industry was the major source of income for the Mexican-Americans, with total receipts of $33 million. Per firm receipts were low for Mexican-American firms, just as was true for Blacks. Limited inroads into the banking industry was also observable for Mexican-Americans. Their representation in the category constituted one-tenth of one percent of all minority firms, even though banking enjoyed one of the highest levels of per firm receipts of $42,727. Mexican-American insurance carriers displayed different revenue characteristics. They had very low average receipts as compared to Mexican-American firms in other industries, while Black insurance carriers had the highest receipts per firm. This results from Mexican-American insurance companies typically being smaller. One possible explanation for lack of representation in the insurance industry is the potentially limited size of the market, that can be attributed to cultural differences of the Mexican-American people. The concept of insurance against illness, accident, or catastrophe is not too clear in the *que-será-será* attitude of the Mexican-American culture. If this does apply, then Mexican-Americans would generally be reluctant to purchase insurance, especially if they are constrained by a limited income and have a short investment time horizon.

In comparing Tables 5-16 and 5-17, we see notable differences in the business characteristics of these two ethnic groups. First of all, per firm receipts of Mexican-American firms were lower than that of Black firms. This can be explained by the fact that because of language, education, and capital barriers, Mexican-Americans have traditionally avoided finance related business ventures. Secondly, the per capita receipts of Mexican-American firms did not show as much dispersion as did those of Black firms. While the range of per capita receipts was $35,000 for the former, the latter showed a range of almost $1.25 million, indicating that there was a greater disparity in revenue distribution among Mexican-Americans in finance, insurance, and real estate. The size factor is also revealed by an examination of the relationship between gross receipts and the number of firms. Unlike Black firms, Mexican-American firms showed a direct relationship between the volume of receipts and the number of firms. Industries with the highest gross receipts for Mexican-American firms were also the ones with the larger number of firms. Industry domination by a few large firms did not characterize the market situation for Mexican-Americans as it did for Blacks. Instead, market volume was generated by a large number of small firms. This also explains the lower per capita figures of Mexican-American firms.

Distribution of Receipts of Black and
Mexican-American Employee-Type Firms

Black firms in real estate are more labor-intensive than firms in other industries, and account for 61 percent of employee-type firms. This approximates the
average for all minority firms, but is notably greater than that of the Spanish-
speaking, which was 47 percent. In most categories Black firms followed the
general trend in employment, while Spanish-speaking firms tended to deviate
from the average distribution pattern.

Real estate employee-type firms generated the maximum receipts in the
Spanish-speaking business community (64 percent). Examining average receipts
for employee-type firms, we see that the receipts of Black firms closely paralleled
those of the all-minority category. The average receipts of Spanish-speaking firms
were below the minority average for the high income generating industries of
banking and insurance. In the lower revenue per capita industries such as real
estate and holding companies, Spanish-speaking firms had average receipts
slightly above those of both Black firms and all-minority firms.

Comparing each category within these three industries, Black banks had the
highest number of employee-type firms among the various ethnic groups. This
was also noticeable in most categories, wherein Black firms were usually above
and Spanish-speaking firms below the all-minority average. The only exceptions
were firms in the securities industry and the insurance agent category, which had

Table 5–18

**Employment Size and Average Revenue Product for Black Employee-Type
Firms in the Finance, Insurance, and Real Estate Industries**

Subindustry Classi- fication and Ranking	Number of Employees	Number of Firms	Employ- ees per Firm	Average Revenue Product (in thousands of dollars)	Annual Total Revenue (in thousands of dollars)
Insurance Carriers	4,146	65	63.8	$32.08	$132,997
Real Estate	2,502	856	2.9	23.16	57,941
Insurance Agents, Brokers, and Services	950	254	3.7	17.41	16,540
Banking	494	30	16.5	49.43	24,418
Credit Agencies Other than Banks	393	86	4.6	31.76	12,482
Combined Real Estate Insurance, etc.	196	63	3.1	23.27	4,561
Security, Commodity Brokers, and Services	167	24	7.0	36.77	6,140
Holding and Other Investment Companies	104	12	8.7	49.83	5,182
Finance, Insurance, and Real Estate Totals	8,952	1,390	6.4	27.91	40,615

a slightly higher proportion of employer firms than all minority firms, in general.

Tables 5-18 and 5-19 show the employment size and average revenue product per employee for Blacks and Mexican Americans. Black firms varied considerably from Mexican-American firms, especially with respect to insurance carriers. Insurance carriers had the largest number of employee-type firms and maintained the largest work force. Both Black and Mexican-American firms in this industry showed a greater employment level, with Black firms showing more use of the paid employee.

Although real estate accounted for the greatest volume of total receipts for Black firms and was the industry which had the largest number of employees, its workers surprisingly generated one of the lowest average revenue products. Black real estate firms had annual receipts of only $23,000 per employee—less than half the revenue product of Black banks and holding companies.

Mexican-American firms in real estate accounted for the largest number of employees (728). Their use of labor was slightly above the other industry categories average of two employees per firm.

Black firms on the average had a lower average revenue product, but higher employment levels per firm. This product-employee inversion may be a form of voluntary accepted disguised unemployment among Black firms. In most cases

Table 5-19

Employment Size and Average Revenue Product for Mexican-American Employee-Type Firms in the Finance, Insurance, and Real Estate Industries

Subindustry Classification and Ranking	Number of Employees	Number of Firms	Employees per Firm	Average Revenue Product (in thousands in dollars)	Annual Total Revenue (in thousands of dollars)
Real Estate	728	337	2.2	$30.96	$ 22,339
Finance, Insurance, and Real Estate Not Allowed by Industry	300	200	1.5	26.00	7,800
Insurance Agents, Brokers, and Services	187	105	1.8	22.04	4,122
Credit Agencies Other than Banks	120	49	2.4	17.13	459
Security, Commodity Brokers, and Services	42	23	1.8	46.29	1,944
Holding and Other Investment Companies	40	7	5.0	59.00	2,635
Combined Real Estate, Insurance, etc.	24	14	1.7	31.21	749
Banking	14	3	4.7	30.79	431
Insurance Carriers[a]	(D)	11	(D)	11.50	126
Finance, Insurance, and Real Estate Totals	1,455	740	1.9	29.07	260,261

[a]Note (D) represents data withheld to avoid disclosing figures for individual companies.

they had a much larger work force than Mexican-Americans. This indicates that the operations in Black firms tend to be overstaffed. As a consequence this reflects itself in a lower average revenue product.

It is estimated that the average employee wage in the finance, insurance, and real estate industries was $5,876 in 1970. This raises some doubts about how many of these firms have the capability to survive. For example, insurance companies owned by Mexican-Americans had receipts of $14,500 per firm. The wage costs for one employee alone account for about 41 percent of the total receipts. Even assuming modest overhead costs, as well as an equivalent wage to the entrepreneur, this still gives the impression that the residual must be bordering on the negative.

Conclusion

The analysis of industry representation and receipts indicates that minority firms in general were heavily concentrated in low income producing industries. Even though Blacks and Spanish-speaking had approximately the same number of firms in the finance, insurance, and real estate industries, Black-owned firms received a larger share of the revenue than the Spanish-speaking firms.[h] This difference was largely due to the number and total receipts of banks, insurance carriers, and credit agencies. With a few exceptions such as holding companies, and security and commodity brokers, Black business ownership was clearly more prevalent than that of the Spanish-speaking.

Latest reports by the Bureau of the Census on minority enterprise disclosed that in 1969–1972 there was a 19 percent increase in the total number of minority firms in the U.S., and their receipts had risen by 56 percent. Compared to this national average, Blacks experienced a 20 percent increase in firms and a 60 percent increase in receipts, while the corresponding figures for the Spanish-speaking were 20 percent and 68 percent, respectively. Although these figures may be interpreted as substantial increases in market volume, it is not clear that we can correctly draw this inference, since some of the additional revenue has been due to a general increase in the aggregate price level during this period.

While the overall number of firms increased along with their receipts, the total number of firms in the finance, insurance, and real estate industries decreased from 28,806 in 1969 to 18,515 in 1972—a drop of 35 percent. Thus the finance-related industries experienced a larger number of casualties during these years of higher interest rates and greater capital scarcity.

---

[h]This should not be viewed as an interethnic revenue distribution problem since neither group competes in the other's market. For the most part, Blacks do not render direct services to the Spanish-speaking, nor vice versa. They may participate in the same industries, but their markets are clearly separate and autonomous from one another. However, what can be considered true for product markets should not necessarily be interpreted as equally true for factor markets.

6 Conclusion

Historically, banks have described themselves as performing a "public trust" and as "serving the community." It is time to examine the reality and implications of these pretensions. It is also time to assess the degree of their compliance with banking and other laws, and to call for broader representation of the community on banks' boards of directors and in the banks' managerial ranks through wiser employment and promotion policies.

—Ralph Nader, 1974[1]

The intention of this study was to investigate the flow of capital in minority communities. Capital was broadly defined as transfers in purchasing power claims—claims that had both short-term and long-term maturities. The series of discussions centering around the relationship between finance and economic development were reviewed. It was found that the arguments are mixed as to whether an a priori judgement can be cast. In examining the conditions under which capital markets are considered well-functioning, it was noted that much emphasis is placed on the solidity of the linkage between savers and investors. With the exception of a few discussions, rarely was the idea introduced that savers and investors as a separate group may possess intergroup socioeconomic differences which relegates some members to disenfranchised fragments of the financial system. The result is that there develops a parasympathetic system of financial markets that remain autonomous from the capital movements that emanate from the established financial centers. Instead of a single linear linkage between savers and lenders, what in effect prevails in the United States, is a multitier system with each tier corresponding to different economic echelons of society. Minorities, because of their racial and poverty status, seldom get beyond the lowest tier of credit, which is the stratum that plays host to pawnbrokers, loan sharks, and ghetto merchants. It is not surprising to see why the relationship between finance and economic development borders on the negative. When organized financial institutions serve solely as depositors for one community, and as sources of investment capital for another, economic growth is retarded for the former and enhanced for the latter. This, in part, describes the nature of the problem that characterizes minority communities. Another dimension of the inner city problem is the internal dearth of financial resources. This can be attributed to the social displacement of unemployment, low income levels, and modest wealth holdings. However, these causal attributes have not evolved fortuitously. Many of these social costs incurred by minorities can be traced to the

147

established order's taste preference for discrimination. What is revealing is not the prevalence of the act of discrimination but rather the magnitude of this social injustice. In recent times, general attention has strayed away from the economic problems of minorities to other issues which the governing society considers more crucial such as environmental and energy conservation. While these are worthwhile concerns, they should not consume society's attention at the expense of the interest in people's need because it is no longer considered "fashionable." We may conserve the landscape for our wild life and find that our cities and its residents have waned from social neglect. For some ghetto households, the conservation of energy translates into the preservation of human energy and economic survival. If progress in alleviating the plight of the minorities is to be made by the turn of the century, then it will be necessary for a bona fide effort to be made in correcting the social costs of the past and *not* to dwell on the voguish self-righteous concern for the potential costs of reverse discrimination, since society at large has not even started to meet its social responsibility to a group whose quest is parity citizenship.

Notes

Chapter 1
The Function of Financial Markets

1. Adam Smith, *Wealth of Nations* (New York: Modern Library, 1966), Book IV, Chapter 2.
2. William J. Baumol, *The Stock Market and Economic Efficiency* (New York: Fordham University Press, 1965), pp. 1–2.
3. Ibid., p. 2.
4. The discussion has benefited from an unpublished paper by R.S. Eckaus, "Notes on Financial Intermediation, Savings and Monetary Controls," which he developed for the Organization of American States while a Visiting Scholar at the University of California at Berkeley.
5. The discussion on the development of financial centers and the section on the influence of banking on economic development draw from Charles P. Kindleberger, "The Formation of Financial Centers: A Study in Comparative Economic History," *Princeton Studies in International Finance,* No. 36, International Finance Section, Department of Economics, Princeton University, 1974. The studies referred to are: Rondo Cameron, ed., *Banking in the Early Stages of Industrialization: A Study in Comparative Economic History,* (New York: Oxford University Press, 1967); ——, *Banking and Economic Development* (New York: Oxford University Press, 1972); A. Gerschenkron, *Economic Backwardness in Historical Perspective* (Cambridge, Mass.: Harvard University Press, 1962); Bert F. Hoselitz, "Entrepreneurship and Capital Formation in France and Britain Since 1700," in *Capital Formation and Economic Growth* (Princeton, N.J.: Princeton University Press for National Bureau of Economic Research, 1956); and Alexander Gerschenkron, "Economic Backwardness in Historical Perspective," in B.F. Hoselitz, ed., *The Progress of Underdeveloped Areas* (Chicago: University of Chicago Press, 1952).
6. James C. Van Horne, *Function and Analysis of Capital Market Rates,* Foundation of Finance Series (Englewood Cliffs, N.J.: Prentice-Hall, 1970), p. 3.
7. Ibid., p. 3.
8. Edward S. Shaw, *Financial Deepening in Economic Development* (New York: Oxford University Press, 1973), p. 3.
9. Ibid., p. 77.
10. Raymond W. Goldsmith, *Financial Structure and Development* (New Haven, Conn.: Yale University Press, 1969), p. 400.

11. Ibid., p. 408.
12. Ronald I. McKinnon, *Money and Capital in Economic Development* (Washington, D.C.: The Brookings Institute, 1973).
13. Gunnar Myrdal, *Economic Theory and Under-Developed Regions* (London: Gerald Duckworth and Co., 1957), pp. 27–28. Aubey has also written an interesting unpublished paper on the "Regional Credit Flows and the Mexican Financial System." Aubey attempts to measure the extent of Myrdal's backwash effect in Mexico.
14. Eckaus, op. cit., p. 1.
15. Cleveland A. Christophe, *Competition in Financial Services,* (New York: First National City Corporation, 1974).
16. Ibid., p. 2.
17. Eckaus, op. cit., pp. 2–3.
18. *Savings and Loan 1973 Fact Book* (Chicago: United States Savings and Loan League, 1973), p. 56.
19. See for example "The Place of Mortgage Banking in the Financial Structure," paper presented to the Commission on Financial Structure and Regulation by the Mortgage Bankers Association, January 1971, p. 25. Also Leo Grebler and J.R. Dominguez, *The Modern Mortgage Company, A Changing Intermediary in a Changing Market* (Advance Mortgage Corporation, 1974).
20. Martin Mayer, *The Bankers* (New York: Weybright and Talling, 1974).
21. "Favorable Trends Seen in Minority Business Growth," *Access* Office of Minority Business Enterprise, U.S. Department of Congress, Washington, D.C., November–December, 1974, p. 7.

Chapter 2
Credit and Credit Markets in the
Inner Cities

1. *Consumer Credit and the Poor,* Hearing Subcommittee on Financial Institutions, Committee on Banking and Currency, United States Senate Ninetieth Congress (Washington, D.C.: U.S. Government Printing Office, April 19, 1968), p. 151.
2. Ivan H. Light, *Ethnic Enterprise in America* (Berkeley: University of California Press, 1972).
3. Verle Johnston, "Financing the Inner City," *Monthly Review,* Federal Reserve Bank of San Francisco, October 1969, p. 199.
4. Charles Sackrey, *The Political Economy of Urban Poverty* (New York: W.W. Norton and Company, 1973), pp. 7–8.
5. Verle Johnston, op. cit., p. 200.
6. Parts of this discussion on risk evaluation come from Sylvia Lane's article, "Sub-marginal Credit Risks: The Comparative Profiles and their Implications," *Journal of Consumer Affairs,* Summer 1971, Vol. 4, No. 1, p. 24.
7. Verle Johnston, op. cit., p. 201.
8. *Consumer Credit and the Poor,* op. cit., p. 1.

9. *Financial Institutions: Reform and the Public Interest,* Staff Report of the Subcommittee on Domestic Finance, Committee on Banking and Currency, House of Representatives, Washington, D.C., August 1973, p. 48.

10. Ibid., p. 22.

11. William D. Bradford, "Minority Financial Institutions, Inner City Economic Development and the Hunt Commission Report," *Review of Black Political Economy,* Vol. 4, No. 3 (Spring 1974), pp. 47–61.

12. The discussion that follows was largely developed from *Consumer Credit and the Poor,* op. cit., pp. 43–94.

Chapter 3
Capital Markets and Nonbank Financial
Intermediaries and the Inner Cities

1. *SBA: What It Is—What It Does* (Washington, D.C., Small Business Administration, August 1974), p. 1.

2. Federal Reserve System, *Financing Small Business,* Report to the Committee on Banking and Currency and the Select Committee on Small Business, United States Congress (Washington, D.C., Government Printing Office, 1958), p. 102.

3. A.D. Kaplan and Paul H. Banner, "Adequacy of Small Business Financing: One View," Federal Reserve System, *Financing Small Business,* op. cit., p. 102.

4. Irving Schweiger, "Adequacy of Small Business Financing: Another View," Federal Reserve System, *Financing Small Business,* op. cit., p. 148.

5. Hans R. Stoll and Anthony J. Curley, "Small Business and the New Issue Market for Equities," *Journal of Financial and Quantitative Analysis,* June 1970, pp. 309–322.

6. W.J. Garvin, "The Small Business Capital Gap: The Special Case of Minority Enterprise," *Journal of Finance,* May 1971, pp. 446–448.

7. Robert C. Kemp, "Minority Business and the New Economy," *Black Enterprise,* October 1972, p. 55.

8. W.J. Garvin, op. cit., pp. 450–456.

9. Timothy Bates, "Trends in Government Promotion of Black Entrepreneurship," *The Review of Black Political Economy,* Vol. 5, No. 2 (Winter 1975), p. 175.

10. Ibid., p. 177.

11. Ibid., p. 178.

12. Ibid., p. 179.

13. Karen DeWitt, "The Small Business Administration," *Black Enterprise,* January 1975, p. 27.

14. George Glass, "A Report on the MESBIC Industry—1974," Report prepared for the Institute for Liberty and Community, Concord, Vermont, January 6, 1975, p. 8.

15. Ibid., p. 10.

16. Ibid., p. 13.

17. Ibid., p. 20.
18. Richard Rosenbloom and John Shank, "Let's Write Off MESBICs," *Harvard Business Review,* September–October, 1970, Vol. 48, No. 5, p. 94.
19. Ibid., p. 92.
20. Ibid., p. 93.
21. *Limited Success of Federally Financed Minority Business in Three Cities,* Report issued by the General Accounting Office, 1973, p. 21.
22. Ibid., p. 19.
23. James K. Brown, "Arcata Investment Company: The Prototype MESBIC," *Conference Board Record,* April 1970, p. 57.
24. Ibid., p. 59.
25. Ibid., p. 60.
26. Ibid., pp. 63–64.
27. Andrew Brimmer and Henry Terrell, "The Potential of Black Capitalism," *Public Policy,* Spring 1971, pp. 289–328.
28. Timothy Bates, "The Potential of Black Capitalism," *Public Policy,* Vol. 21 No. 1 Winter 1973, pp. 135–148.
29. Alfred Osborne, Jr., and Michael Granfield, "The Potential of Black Capitalism in Perspective," an unpublished paper written at the University of California, Los Angeles, 1974.
30. Ibid., p. 21.
31. Ibid., p. 23.
32. Ibid., p. 25.
33. George Glass, op. cit., pp. 25–30.

Chapter 4
Commercial Banking in the Inner Cities

1. "Favorable Trends Seen in Minority Business Growth," *Access,* Office of Minority Business Enterprise, U.S. Department of Commerce, Washington, D.C., November–December, 1974, p. 7.
2. "Industrial Bankers Joining Drive to Aid Minority Firms," *Commerce Today,* August, 1971, p. 24. Used with permission of Warren, Gorham, and Lamont, Inc., Boston, Mass.
3. Frederick D. Sturdivant, "Business and the Mexican American Community," *California Management Review,* Spring 1969, p. 78.
4. Charles Allen Whitney, "Black Banks Are Good Business," *Bankers Magazine* Spring 1969, p. 24.
5. Ibid., p. 21.
6. Franklin A. Thomas, "Black Power and the Banks," *Bankers Magazine,* Winter 1971, p. 22.
7. Charles Allen Whitney, "Black Banks Are Good Business," op. cit., p. 21.
8. Charlotte P. Hall, "History of the NBA . . . A Look Into the Past," *Moving Forward into the 1970's,* National Bankers Association, Washington, D.C., 1971, pp. 2–3.
9. Andrew F. Brimmer, "The Black Banks: An Assessment of Performance

and Prospects," *Journal of Finance,* Vol. 26, No. 2 (May 1971), p. 380, and John T. Boorman, *New Minority-Owned Commercial Banks: A Comparative Analysis,* Washington, D.C.: Federal Deposit Insurance Corporation, August 1973, p. 4.

10. Martin Mayer, *The Bankers* (New York: Weybright and Talley, 1974), p. 337. Copyright © 1974 by Martin Mayer. From the book THE BANKERS, published by Weybright and Talley, a division of the David McKay Company Inc. Used with permission of the publishers.

11. "Blacks Build Up Their Bank Power," *Business Week,* December 5, 1970, p. 92.

12. "Negro Business Feels Stresses of Success," *Business Week,* April 9, 1966, p. 74.

13. Ibid., p. 74.

14. "Minority Banking Grows in Washington," *Access,* Office of Minority Business Enterprise, U.S. Department of Commerce, Washington, D.C., November–December, 1974, p. 4.

15. "The Vanishing American," *Trust and Estates,* November 1969, p. 1061.

16. Gordon Mitchell, "Bank Helps Indians Become Entrepreneurs," *Banking,* August 1960, p. 148.

17. Andrew Brimmer, "The Black Banks: An Assessment of Performance and Prospects, op. cit., p. 399.

18. Ibid., p. 381.

19. Ibid., p. 401.

20. "Six Minority Banks Chartered in 1971," *Outlook,* Office of Minority Business Enterprise, U.S. Department of Commerce, Washington, D.C., May 1972, p. 8.

21. Harold R. Algar and Richard Linyard, "Asset Management in a Profit Oriented Black Bank," paper presented at 45th Annual Convention of the National Bankers Association, Houston, Texas, October 12, 1972. H.R. Algar and R. Linyard are executive officers of the Seaway National Bank of Chicago which was one of the banks in Brimmer's test sample.

22. Lyle E. Gramley, *A Study of Scale Economies in Banking,* Research Department, Federal Reserve Bank of Kansas City, June 1969, p. 5.

Chapter 5
Capital Flows and the Economics of
the Inner Cities

1. Frank G. Davis, *The Economics of Black Community Development,* Chicago: Markham Publishing Company, 1972) pp. 38–42.

2. Dunbar S. McLaurin and Cyril D. Tyson, "The GHEDIPLAN for Economic Development," *Black Economic Development,* (Englewood Cliffs, N.J.: Prentice Hall, 1969) pp. 126–137.

3. Bennett Harrison, *Ghetto Economic Development,* unpublished manuscript written under a grant from the U.S. Office of Economic Opportunity for the Project on Economics of Discrimination, University of Maryland, 1972.

4. Theodore L. Cross, *Black Capitalism: Strategy for Business in the Ghetto,* (New York: Atheneum, 1969) p. 211. © 1969 by Theodore L. Cross.

5. Thomas Vietorisz and Bennett Harrison, *The Economic Development of Harlem,* (New York: Frederick A. Praeger, 1970) p. 39.

6. James Heilbrun and Roger R. Conant, "The Profitability and Size of a Firm as Evidence of Dualism in the Black Ghetto," *Urban Affairs Quarterly,* March 1972, p. 264.

7. Alber J. Reiss, *Minority Entrepreneurship,* Office of Planning, Research, and Analysis, Small Business Administration, Washington, D.C., 1969, p. 9.

8. Andrew Brimmer and Henry Terrell, "The Economic Potential of Black Capitalism," *Publid Policy,* Spring 1971, p. 304.

9. Charles Tate, "Brimmer and Black Capitalism: An Analysis," *Review of Black Political Economy,* Spring/Summer 1970, pp. 84–90.

10. Richard H. Leftwich and Ansel M. Sharp, *Economics of Social Issues* (Dallas, Texas: Business Publications, 1974), p. 110.

11. Roy F. Lee, *Black Business Development,* New York State School of Industrial and Labor Relations, 1973.

12. Timothy Bates, "The Potential of Black Capitalism," *Public Policy,* Winter 1974. Reprinted with permission from *Public Policy.*

13. Bennett Harrison, *Ghetto Economic Development,* op. cit., pp. 61–65.

14. Bennett Harrison, op. cit., pp. 65–68.

15. Andrew F. Brimmer, "Economic Development in the Black Community," *Public Interest,* No. 34 (Winter 1974), p. 147.

16. "A Piece of the Action," *Manpower,* September 1971, p. 8.

17. Andrew F. Brimmer, "Economic Development in the Black Community, op. cit., p. 153.

18. "Problems Related to the Training of Spanish-Speaking Americans," U.S. Department of Labor, Manpower Administration, Washington, D.C., an unpublished paper prepared for the 15th Meeting of the National Manpower Advisory Committee's Subcommittee on Training, November 10, 1972, pp. 3–10.

19. Henry S. Terrell, "Wealth Accumulation of Black and White Families: The Empirical Evidence," *Journal of Finance, Papers and Proceedings,* Vol. 26, No. 2 (May, 1971), pp. 363–377.

20. Marcus Alexis, "Discussion: Wealth Accumulation of Black and White Families: The Empirical Evidence," *Journal of Finance Papers and Proceedings,* Vol. 26, No. 2 (May 1971), p. 460.

21. Milton Friedman, *A Theory of the Consumption Function,* (Princeton, N.J.: Princeton University Press, 1957), pp. 20–26.

22. Milton Friedman, op. cit., p. 37.

23. Henry S. Terrell, op. cit., p. 369.

24. Marcus Alexis, op. cit., p. 458.

25. "The Census Bureau Reports a Rise in Education," *Access,* Office of Minority Business Enterprise, U.S. Department of Commerce, Washington, D.C., May–June 1975, p. 13.

26. Phillip D. Ortego, "The Education of Mexican Americans," *The Chicanos: Mexican-American Voices,* 1971, edited by Rudwig and Santibanez, p. 158.

27. Niles M. Hansen, "Improving Economic Opportunity for Mexican-Americans," *Economics and Business Bulletin,* Fall 1969, p. 2.

Chapter 6
Conclusion

1. David Leinsdorf and Donald Etra, *Citibank,* (New York: Grossman Publishers, 1974), p. xiii.

Bibliography

Atkinson, Thomas R. *The Pattern of Financial Asset Ownership.* Princeton, N.J.: Princeton University Press (1956).

Aubey, Robert. "Regional Credit Flows and the Mexican Financial System." Unpublished paper from the International Business Research Center, University of Wisconsin, Madison, Wisconsin (1971).

Baker, Lea B., Richard A. Wald, and Rita Zamora. *Economic Aspects of Mexican and Mexican-American Urban Households.* Published by the Institute for Business and Economic Research. San Jose State College (1971).

Bates, Timothy. "Financing Black Enterprise." *Journal of Finance,* Vol. 29, No. 3. (June 1974).

Bates, Timothy. "Trends in Government Promotion of Black Entrepreneurship." *The Review of Black Political Economy,* Vol. 5, No. 2 (Winter 1975), pp. 175–284.

Baumol, William J. *The Stock Market and Economic Efficiency.* New York: Fordham University Press (1965).

Bell, Frederick W. and Murphy, Neil B. *Economics of Scale in Commercial Banking.* Federal Reserve Bank of Boston (August 1967).

Benston, George J. "How We Can Learn From Past Bank Failures," *The Bankers Magazine,* Vol. 158, No. 1 (Winter 1975), pp. 19–26.

Blume, Marshall E., Jean Crockett and Irwin Friend et al. "Stock Ownership in the United States: Characteristics and Trends." *Survey of Current Business,* Vol. 54, No. 11 (November 1974).

Boorman, John. *New Minority-Owned Commercial Banks: A Comparative Analysis.* Washington, D.C.: Federal Deposit Insurance Corporation (1973).

Bowen, Howard R. *The Interpretation of Voting in the Allocation of Resources.* Homewood, Illinois: Richard D. Irwin (1969).

Bradford, William D. "Minority Financial Institutions, Inner City Economic Development and the Hunt Commission Report." *The Review of Black Political Economy,* Vol. 4, No. 3 (Spring 1974), pp. 47–61.

Bratter, Herbert. "Increasing Minority Bank Deposits." *Banking* (November 1974), p. 74.

"Briefs on Minority Business." *Access,* Office of Minority Business Enterprise, Washington, D.C.: U.S. Department of Commerce (March–April 1975), pp. 13–14.

Brimmer, A.F. "The Black Banks: An Assessment of Performance and Prospects." *Journal of Finance,* Vol. 26, No. 2 (May 1971), pp. 379–405.

Bryan, Lowell, L. "Put a Price on Credit Lines." *The Banker's Magazine,* Vol. 157, No. 3 (Summer 1974), pp. 44–49.

"Burger King Commits $38 Million to Minority Enterprise." *Access,* Office

of Minority Business Enterprise, Washington, D.C.: U.S. Department of
Commerce (November –December 1973), p. 10.

Business Conditions. Federal Reserve Bank of Chicago (September 1973).

Cacy, J.A. "Commercial Bank Profitability: 1961–1971." *Monthly Review,*
Federal Reserve Bank of Kansas City (September–October 1972), pp.
3–12.

Cameron, Rondo. *Banking and Economic Development.* New York: Oxford
University Press (1972).

——, ed., *Banking in the Early States of Industrialization: A Study in Comparative Economic History.* New York: Oxford University Press (1967).

——. *Economic Backwardness in Historical Perspective.* Cambridge, Mass.:
Harvard University Press (1962).

Christophe, Cleveland A. *Competition in Financial Services.* New York: First
National City Corporation (1974).

Clifford, John T. *"The Unhealthy Condition of Bank Statements."* The
Bankers Magazine, Vol. 158, No. 1 (Winter 1975), pp. 90–95.

Consumer Credit and the Poor. Hearing Subcommittee on Banking and Currency, United States Senate Ninetieth Congress. Washington, D.C.: U.S.
Government Printing Office (April 19, 1968).

Cooper, Richard. "Efficient Capital Markets and the Quantity Theory of
Money." *Journal of Finance,* Vol. 29, No. 3 (June 1974).

Copeland, Morris A. *A Study of Money Flows in the United States.* New York:
National Bureau of Economic Research, (1952).

Crosse, Howard O. "Capital Adequacy." *The Bankers Magazine* (Summer
1975), p. 83.

Davis, Frank G. *The Economics of Black Community Development.* Chicago:
Markham Publishing Company (1972).

DeWitt, Karen. "The Small Business Administration." *Black Enterprise,* Vol. 5,
No. 6 (January 1975), pp. 25–27.

"The Director's Corner." *Access,* Office of Minority Business Enterprise,
Washington, D.C.: U.S. Department of Commerce (May–June, 1973), p. 2.

"Domestic Business Report." *Commerce Today* (January 25, 1971), p. 108.

Dougall, Herbert E. *Capital Markets and Institutions.* Englewood Cliffs, N.J.:
Prentice-Hall (1970).

Duker, Jacob M., and T. Gregory Morton. "Black Owned Banks: Issues and
Recommendations." *California Management Review,* Vol. 17, No. 1 (Fall
1974).

Eckaus, Richard S. "Notes on Financial Intermediation, Savings and Monetary
Controls." Unpublished paper developed for the Organization of American
States, University of California, Berkeley, 1972.

Emeka, Mauris L. "Some Common Problems of Black Banks in 1972." *The
Review of Black Political Economy,* Vol. 3, No. 3 (Spring 1973), pp. 100–
116.

Essays on Southern Economic Growth. Readings in Southern Finance, No. 4.
Selected Articles from the Monthly Review of the Federal Reserve Bank
of Atlanta (1960–1961).

"Favorable Trends Seen in Minority Business Growth." *Access,* Office of

Minority Business Enterprise, Washington, D.C.: U.S. Department of
Commerce, (November–December, 1974), pp. 6–7.

Feldman, A. and Kirman. "Fairness and Envy." *The American Economic
Review,* Vol. 64, No. 6 (December 1974).

Financial Institutions: Reform and the Public Interest. Staff Report of the
Subcommittee on Domestic Finance, Committee on Banking and Currency,
House of Representatives, Washington, D.C. (August 1973.)

Financing Small Business. Report by the Federal Reserve System to the Committee on Banking and Currency and the Select Committee on Small
Business, U.S. Congress, Washington, D.C.: Government Printing Office
(1958).

The Flow of Funds Approach to Social Accounting. Princeton, N.J.: Princeton
University Press (1962).

Galbraith, John Kenneth. *Economies and the Public Purpose.* Boston: Houghton
Mifflin Company (1973).

Garvin, W.J. "The Small Business Capital Gap: The Special Case of Minority
Enterprise." *Journal of Finance,* Vol. 26, No. 2 (May 1971), pp. 445–457.

Gerschenkron, Alexander. "Economic Backwardness in Historical Perspective."
In B.F. Hoselitz, ed., *The Progress of Underdeveloped Areas.* Chicago:
University of Chicago Press (1952).

Glass, George. *A Report on the MESBIC Industry–1974.* Report prepared for
the Institute for Liberty and Community, Concord, Vermont (January 6,
1975).

Goldsmith, Raymond W. *Financial Structure and Development.* New Haven,
Conn.: Yale University Press (1969).

Gramley, Lyle E. *A Study of Scale Economies in Banking.* Federal Reserve
Bank of Kansas City. Kansas City, Mo. (1969).

Grebler, Leo, Joan W. Moore, and Ralph Guzman. *The Mexican American
People.* New York: The Free Press (1970).

Grebler, Leo and John R. Dominguez. *The Modern Mortgage Company, A
Changing Intermediary in a Changing Market.* Unpublished paper sponsored
by Advance Mortgage Corporation (December 1974).

Greenwald, Carol S. "Banks Should Stop Discriminating Against Women in
Employment." *The Bankers Magazine,* Vol. 157, No. 3 (Summer 1974),
pp. 74–79.

Guttentag, Jack M. "Banking Structure and Performance." *Economics of
Scale.* New York University Graduate School of Business Administration,
Institute of Finance (February, 1967).

Haddad, William F. and Douglas Pugh, eds. *Black Economic Development.*
Englewood Cliffs, N.J.: Prentice Hall (1969).

Harrison, Bennett, *Ghetto Economic Development.* Paper written with the
support from the U.S. Office of Economic Opportunity, Massachusetts
Institute of Technology (November, 1972).

Hoselitz, Bert F. "Enterpreneurship and Capital Formation in France and
Britain Since 1700." In *Capital Formation and Economic Growth.* Prince-
ton, N.J.: Princeton University Press for National Bureau of Economic
Research (1956).

Irons, D.F. "Black Banking Problems and Prospects." *Journal of Finance,*
    Vol. 26, No. 2 (May 1971), pp. 405–407.
Jacquette, Lee F. "Public Interest Investment by Banks." *The Bankers Magazine,*
    Vol. 157, No. 4 (Autumn 1974), pp. 115–122.
Johnston, Verle. "Financing the Inner City." *Monthly Review,* Federal Reserve
    Bank of San Francisco (October 1969), p. 199.
Kalish, Lionel and R. Alton Gilbert. "The Influence of Bank Regulation on
    the Operating Efficiency of Commercial Banks." *Journal of Finance,*
    Vol. 28, No. 5 (December 1973).
Kapp, William K. *The Social Costs of Private Business.* New York: Schocken
    Books (1950).
Kemp, Robert C. "Minority Business and the New Economy." *Black Enterprise,*
    Vol. 3, No. 3 (October 1972), pp. 55–58.
Kilpatrick, James J. "The Peril of Success." *Los Angeles Times* (June 19, 1975),
    Part II, p. 7.
Kindleberger, Charles P. "The Formation of Financial Centers: A Study in
    Comparative Economic History." *Princeton Studies in International
    Finance,* No. 36. Princeton, N.J.: Princeton University Press (1974).
Lee, Chung H. "Information Costs and Markets." *Economic Inquiry,* Vol. 12,
    No. 4 (December 1974), pp. 460–475.
Leinsdorf, David and Donald Etra. *Citibank.* New York: Grossman Publishers
    (1974).
Leontief, Wassily. "Theoretical Assumptions and Nonobserved Facts." *American Economic Review,* Vol. 61, No. 1 (March 1971), pp. 1–7.
Life Insurance Fact Book 1974. Institute of Life Insurance, New York (1974).
Light, Ivan H. *Ethnic Enterprise in America.* Berkeley: University of California
    Press, (1972).
Limited Success of Federally Financed Minority Business in Three Cities. Report
    to the Congress by the Comptroller General of the United States, General
    Accounting Office (1973).
Little, Dennis L. "Social Indicators and Public Policy: Some Unanswered
    Questions." *Futures* (February 1975), pp. 41–51.
The Los Angeles Market: Variations in Buying Patterns Between Spanish Speaking and Non-Spanish Speaking Households. Marketing and Research
    Counselors Inc., Dallas, Texas (1974).
McKinnon, Ronald I. *Money and Capital in Economic Development.* Washington, D.C.: The Brookings Institute (1973).
Maisel, Sherman J. "The Economic and Finance Literature and Decision Making."
    Journal of Finance, Vol. 29, No. 2 (May 1974), p. 318.
Marsh, James. "Viewing the Loss Experience on Minority Enterprise Loans."
    The Bankers Magazine (Winter 1971).
Marshall, Ray. "The Economics of Racial Discrimination: A Survey." *Journal
    of Economic Literature,* Vol. 12, No. 3 (September, 1974) pp. 849–871.
Mayer, Martin. *The Bankers.* New York: Weybright and Talling (1974).
Minority Enterprise and Expanded Ownership: Blueprint for the 70's. Presi-

dent's Advisory Council on Minority Business Enterprise, Washington, D.C.,
    (June 1971).

Minority Owned Businesses 1969. MB-1, Bureau of the Census, U.S. Depart-
    ment of Commerce (August 1971).

Moving Forward into the 1970's. National Bankers Association, Washington,
    D.C. (1971).

Myrdal, Gunnar. *Economic Theory and Under-developed Regions.* London,
    England: Gerald Duckworth and Co. (1957).

National Minority Business Directory 1973. National Minority Business Cam-
    paign. Minneapolis, Minn. (1974).

Novelline, William T. "Where Bank Profits go from Here." *The Bankers Magazine,*
    Vol. 158, No. 1 (Winter 1975), pp. 64–71.

Osborne, Alfred, Jr., and Michael Granfield. "The Potential of Black Capitalism
    in Perspective." Unpublished paper written at the University of California,
    Los Angeles (1974).

"The Place of Mortgage Banking in the Financial Structure." Paper presented
    to the Commission on Financial Structure and Regulation, Mortgage
    Bankers Association, Washington, D.C. (1971).

Ritchie, Robert. "Minority Owned Banks: Profit Picture Improving." *Business
    Review,* Federal Reserve Bank of Philadelphia (1974).

Robinson, Marshall A., Herbert C. Morton, and James D. Calderwood. *An
    Introduction to Economic Reasoning.* Garden City, N.Y.: Anchor Books
    (1962).

Rosenbloom, Richard, and John Shank. "Let's Write Off MESBICS." *Harvard
    Business Review,* Vol. 48, No. 5 (September–October, 1970), pp. 90–97.

SBA: What It Is—What It Does. Small Business Administration, Washington,
    D.C.: U.S. Department of Commerce (August 1974).

Sackrey, Charles. *The Political Economy of Urban Poverty.* New York: W.W.
    Norton and Company (1973).

Savings and Loan 1973 Fact Book. Chicago: United States Savings and Loan
    League (1973).

Scherer, F.M. *Industrial Market Structure and Economic Performance.* Chicago:
    Rand McNally and Company (1970).

Schmidt, Susan Bies. "Determinants of Commercial Bank Growth." *Review,*
    Federal Reserve Bank of St. Louis, Vol. 53, No. 12 (December 1971),
    pp. 11–19.

Shaw, Edward S. *Financial Deepening in Economic Development.* New York:
    Oxford University Press (1973).

Sinkey, Joseph F. "The Way Problem Banks Perform." *The Bankers Magazine,*
    Vol. 157, No. 4 (Autumn 1974), pp. 40–52.

"Small Bank Portfolio Behavior." *Business Conditions* (March 1973), pp. 3–10.

Smith, Adam. *An Inquiry Into the Nature and Causes of the Wealth of Nations.*
    Vol. II, Tenth Edition, London, England: A. Strahan (1802).

*Social Indicators 1973: Selected Statistics on Social Conditions and Trends in
    the United States.* Statistical Policy Division, Office of Management and

Budget. Washington, D.C.: Social and Economic Statistics Administration, U.S. Department of Commerce, Government Printing Office (1973).

Soldofsky, Robert M. *Institutional Holdings of Common Stock 1900-2000.* Michigan Business Studies, Vol. 28, No. 3, Ann Arbor: University of Michigan (1971).

Stans, Maurice H. *Progress of the Minority Business Enterprise Program.* Washington, D.C.: U.S. Department of Commerce (January 1972), pg. 98.

Stigler, George J. *The Theory of Price.* New York: The McMillan Co. (1952).

Stiglitz, J.E. "The Theory of 'Screening,' Education and the Distribution of Income." *The American Economic Review,* Vol. 65, No. 3 (June 1975).

Texas Banking: Red Book 1974. Bankers Digest, Inc., Red Book Division, Dallas, Texas (1974).

Thieblot, Armand J. Jr. and Linda Pickthorne Fletcher, *Negro Employment in Finance.* Industrial Research Unit Wharton School of Finance and Commerce, Philadelphia, Penn.: University of Pennsylvania (1970).

Tyrrell, Gerald G. *A Positive Approach to Financing Black Business.* Boston, Mass.: Financial Publishing Co. (1972).

Van Horne, James C. *Function and Analysis of Capital Market Rates.* Foundation of Finance Series, Englewood Cliffs, N.J.: Prentice-Hall (1970).

Weston, Fred J. *Managerial Finance.* Fifth Edition, Hinsdale, Ill.: The Dryden Press (1975).

"When A Bank Tries to Change Neighborhoods." *Business Week,* No. 2249 (October 7, 1972), pp. 95–96.

"Where Will Minority Banks Get Additional Capital Funds?" *Banking* (August 1971), pp. 26–27.

Wise, D.A. "Academic Achievement and Job Performance." *The American Economic Review,* Vol. 65, No. 3 (June 1975).

Index

About the Author

John R. Dominguez received the B.A. in Economics from the University of Southern California and the Ph.D. in Economics from the Massachusetts Institute of Technology. He is an Associate Professor of Economics at the University of California at Los Angeles.

He is the author of the books *Devaluation and Futures Markets* and *Venture Capital* as well as a number of articles in economic journals.

Related Lexington Books

Conroy, Michael E., *The Challenge of Urban Economic Development,* 144 pp., 1975.

Greene, Kenneth V., Neenan, William B., and Scott, Claudia D., *Fiscal Interactions in a Metropolitan Area,* 288 pp., 1974.

Phares, Donald and Greytak, David, *Municipal Output and Performance in New York City,* In Press.

Rabinovitz, Francine F. and Siembieda, William J., *Minorities in the Suburbs,* In Press.

Schaffer, Richard L., *Income Flows in Urban Poverty Areas,* 128 pp., 1973.

Sexton, Donald E., Jr., *Groceries in the Ghetto,* 160 pp., 1973.

Steiss, Alan Walter, *Urban Systems Dynamics,* 352 pp., 1974.

Steiss, Alan Walter, Dickey, John W., Phelps, Bruce, and Harvey, Michael, *Dynamic Change and the Urban Ghetto,* 144 pp., 1975.

Zehner, Robert B. and Chapin, F. Stuart, Jr., *Across the City Line: A White Community in Transition,* 272 pp., 1974.